Virginia Woolf

Virginia Woolf

Dorothy Brewster

London

GEORGE ALLEN & UNWIN LTD

PRINTED IN GREAT BRITAIN
BY JOHN DICKENS & CO. LTD., NORTHAMPTON

To my friends

LOUISE DAVIDSON *and* LILLIAN GILKES

Acknowledgments

The author gratefully acknowledges the permission granted by Mr. Leonard Woolf and the Hogarth Press to quote from the works of Virginia Woolf, and from his autobiography, *Sowing*. To both Mr. Woolf and to Miss Daphne Sanger of London, she is indebted for the privilege of quoting extracts from unpublished letters of Virginia Woolf in Miss Sanger's possession.

Contents

1. Biography

The City, the Sea, and the Library

VIRGINIA STEPHEN, born in London, January 26, 1882, was one of the younger children of a distinguished literary family. Her father, Leslie Stephen, editor of the *Dictionary of National Biography* and of the *Cornhill Magazine*, was the author of critical, biographical, and philosophical essays, and the friend of scholars and men of letters during a brilliant period of English literature. His first wife was Thackeray's daughter; his second, the mother of Julian Thoby, Adrian, Vanessa, and Virginia, was Julia Jackson, widow of Herbert Duckworth, with three children of that marriage. She was one of six sisters whose beauty, writes Leonard Woolf in *Sowing*, was legendary; three photographs of her are included in *Victorian Photographs* by Julia Margaret Cameron; Virginia Woolf's introduction contains some amusing anecdotes about her great-grandfather, James Pattle of the Bengal Civil Service, and his French wife. The Stephen family in the London house at Hyde Park Gate must have resembled the Ramsays in *To the Lighthouse*, with the older and younger boys and girls. Virginia Woolf in her fiction and her *Diary* seems very much at ease with young people of both sexes. The tie with her sister Vanessa was very close, and with her brother Thoby, whose sudden death at the age of twenty-five, during a holiday in Greece in 1906, had a profound effect upon her work. The sudden extinction of promise is the story of Rachel in *The Voyage Out*, of Jacob in *Jacob's Room*, and of Perceval in *The Waves*.

"Denham," writes Mrs. Woolf in *Night and Day*, "had accused Katharine Hilbery of belonging to one of the most distinguished families in England." Several names (all fictitious) are mentioned that "seem to prove that intellect is a possession which can be tossed from one member of a certain group to another almost indefinitely." In the Hilbery connection there are judges, admirals, explorers, generals, writers; and in fact, English society being what it is, "no very great merit is required, once you bear a well-known name, to put you into a position where it is easier on the whole to be eminent than obscure." And (the feminist touch) "even the daughters, even in the nineteenth century, are apt to become people of importance—philanthropists and educationalists if they are spinsters, and the wives of distinguished men if they marry." [1] Noel Annan (*Leslie Stephen* [2]) describes the emergence of an intellectual aristocracy in Victorian society, with certain families establishing an intellectual ascendancy and sharing the spoils of the professional and academic worlds among their children. He lists the Huxleys, Arnolds, Trevelyans, Macaulays, Darwins, Wedgwoods, Venns, and Stephens. Sir Leslie Stephen's brother was a jurist and Anglo-Indian administrator; his niece, Katharine Stephen, was the Principal of Newnham College. Victorian families were large, offering a wide choice of intermarriages. There were ten children in the Strachey family, close friends of the Stephens. Macaulays and Stephens were spiritual descendants of the Clapham Sect —"a circle of wealthy Evangelicals who practised what Wesley had preached, and spread the gospel of what was to become the widest religious movement in Victorian England,"

[1] *Night and Day*, Chap. III.
[2] Pp. 2–3.

philanthropic and humanitarian as well as ethical and religious. The Clapham Sect, to which Leslie Stephen adhered in his early years, regarded the family as the natural center of worship, and Noel Annan states that Stephen "founds the moral health of society upon the institution of the family in his *Science of Ethics*" (p. 118). This Victorian intellectual class measured its relations with other classes on the basis of mental and moral attributes, but it could—as Mr. Annan points out—be called aristocratic "because its members feel ultimately secure; secure in that they are satisfied that their standard of values transcends all others; secure in that they are well to do."

In 1932, on the centenary of her father's birth, Virginia Woolf wrote for *The Times* "The Philosopher at Home: A Daughter's Memories." He was fifty years old when she was born, and the great days of his life were over—his athletic feats on the river and in the mountains. "Relics of them were to be found lying about the house—the silver cup on the study mantelpiece; the rusty alpenstocks that leant against the bookcase in the corner; and to the end of his days he would speak of great climbers and explorers with a peculiar mixture of admiration and envy." He had to content himself with "pottering about the Swiss valleys or taking a stroll across the Cornish moors." Although he had already published his *History of English Thought in the Eighteenth Century* and *The Science of Ethics*, he still wrote daily and methodically in his study at the top of the house, books scattered around him in a circle. She recalls how he would take his hat and his stick and "calling for his dog and his daughter, he would stride off into Kensington Gardens, where he had walked as a little boy, where his brother Fitzjames and he had made beautiful bows to young Queen Victoria and she had swept them a curtsey, and so, round the Serpentine, to Hyde Park Corner, where he had once saluted the great Duke himself; and so home. He was not then in the least 'alarming'; he was very simple, very confiding; and his silence, though one might last unbroken from the Round Pond to the Marble Arch, was curiously full of meaning, as if he were thinking half aloud, about poetry and philosophy and people he had known." The habit of walking through the parks and squares and streets of London, established thus early with her father, remained one of the most persistent of Mrs. Woolf's occupations, fruitful of ideas for her work, of background for her novels, and the subject of one of her most charming essays—"Street Haunting." [3]

That Sir Leslie Stephen could be "alarming" in certain ways may be inferred from the behavior of Mr. Ambrose (*The Voyage Out*) and Mr. Ramsay (*To the Lighthouse*). But his daughter in her memories stresses the atmosphere of freedom in their family life—"the right to think one's own thoughts and to follow one's own pursuits," and choose one's own profession. He did not like to see women smoke, but the freedom his daughters had in other ways was worth thousands of cigarettes. Even today, she notes (1932), some parents might object to allowing a girl of fifteen the free run of a large and quite unexpurgated library. Though her father referred shyly to "certain facts," he yet said, "read what you like"; and his only lesson in the art of reading was "to read what one liked because one liked it, never to pretend to admire what one did not"; and the only lesson in the art of writing, "to write in the fewest possible words, as clearly as possible, exactly what one meant." The art of writing, recalled Mrs. Woolf in her *Diary* (Dec. 19, 1938), had been "absorbing ever since I was a little creature, scribbling a story in the manner of Hawthorne on the green plush sofa in the drawing room at St. Ives while the grown-ups dined."

What did she read in those early years and what did she write? A *Writer's Diary* (Dec. 8, 1929) records: "It was the Elizabethan prose writers I loved first and most wildly, stirred

3 Reprinted in *The Death of the Moth.*

by Hakluyt, which father lugged home for me—I think of it with some sentiment—father tramping over the Library with his little girl sitting at H.P.G. [Hyde Park Gate] in mind. He must have been 65; I 15 or 16 then; and why I don't know but I became enraptured, though not exactly interested, but the sight of the large yellow page entranced me. I used to dream of those obscure adventurers and no doubt practised their style in my copybook." To this early fascination may be traced the episode of the Russian princess in *Orlando* and the scenery along the South American river in *The Voyage Out*. "I was then writing," the *Diary* continues, "a long picturesque essay upon the Christian religion, I think; called Religio Laici, I believe, proving that man has need of a God; but the God was described in process of change; and I also wrote a history of Women; and a history of my own family— all very longwinded and Elizabethan in style." God, Women, Family: an interesting assortment for Leslie Stephen's young daughter; for Stephen was by then an agnostic, who believed profoundly in "the worth of human relationships"; and as for Women, the future feminist was to write *A Room of One's Own* and *Three Guineas*.

When she was working on *To the Lighthouse*, Virginia Woolf notes in the *Diary* (Nov. 28, 1928) that her father would have been ninety-six. "His life would have entirely ended mine. . . . No writing, no books: inconceivable. . . . I used to think of him and mother daily; but writing *The Lighthouse* laid them in my mind. And now he comes back sometimes, but differently. (I believe this to be true—that I was obsessed by them both, unhealthily; and writing of them was a necessary act.) He comes back now more as a contemporary. I must read him some day." A dozen years later (Dec. 22, 1940) she notes: "How beautiful they were, these old people—I mean father and mother—how simple, how clear, how untroubled. I have been dipping into old letters and father's memoirs. He loved her: oh and was so candid and reasonable and transparent. How serene and gay even, their life reads to me: no mud; no whirlpools. And so human—with the children and the little hum and song of the nursery.... Nothing turbulent; nothing involved; no introspection." How close to the originals were the portraits of Mr. and Mrs. Ramsay? Her sister Vanessa said that Mrs. Ramsay was "an amazing portrait of mother" (*Diary*, May 16, 1927). Leonard Woolf, who knew Leslie Stephen and heard a great deal about him from his children, thinks there are traces of unfairness; his exactingness and sentimentality were exaggerated—due to "a complicated variety of the Oedipus complex" (*Sowing*). Noel Annan (*Leslie Stephen*) considers Mr. Ramsay an accurate portrait. If anyone still reads Meredith's *Egoist*, it is said that Stephen is the model for Vernon Whitford.

Visitors at the house at Hyde Park Gate were many and distinguished. James Russell Lowell, minister to the Court of St. James in the 1880's, stood godfather to Virginia—or, as Stephen preferred to put it, stood in "quasi-sponsorial relation." Virginia must often have had the experience of her heroine Katharine Hilbery, who "in her childhood, was again and again brought down into the drawing-room to receive the blessing of some awful distinguished old man, who sat, even to her childish eye, somewhat apart, all gathered together and clutching a stick, unlike an ordinary visitor in her father's own arm-chair, and her father himself was there, unlike himself, too, a little excited and very polite." Thomas Hardy, when Mrs. Woolf had tea with him in 1926, recalled seeing her, "or it might have been my sister, but he thought it was me, in my cradle" (*Diary*, July 25). Henry James was a frequent guest of the Stephen family when the children were young. When he came to tea he used to tilt his chair back as he talked; and the children watched fascinated, fearing and hoping that it would tilt backwards far enough to deposit him on the floor—as it did once; but he was unhurt and undismayed, and after a moment completed his sentence. James felt, years later, when he saw the Stephen girls at Rye, that they and their friends were not quite up to the ladylike standard which belonged to Hyde Park Gate (L. Woolf, *Sowing*, 107–109). But they were very ladylike when Leonard Woolf first met them, at a tea party in their brother Thoby's rooms at Cambridge, chaperoned by their cousin, the Principal of Newnham. It was a summer afternoon, Vanessa and Virginia in white dresses, with large hats, and parasols, on the surface "the most Victorian of Victorian young ladies," whose beauty "literally took one's breath away." Yet there was a look in their eyes that warned the observer to be cautious, belying the demureness, "a look of great intelligence, hypercritical, sarcastic, satirical" (*Ibid.*, 183 f.).

The death of her mother when Virginia was thirteen was the first of the losses that affected her deeply. Her half sister, Stella Duckworth, took charge of the household for several years, till Vanessa Stephen was old enough, and then Stella married—dying soon after the birth of her first baby. In the "Time Passes" interlude of *To the Lighthouse*, there is parenthetical mention of the deaths of Mrs. Ramsay and her daughter Prue. "(Mr. Ramsay, stumbling along a passage one dark night, stretched his arms out, but Mrs. Ramsay having died rather suddenly the night before, his arms, though stretched out, remained empty.)" The death of Mrs. Pargiter in *The Years* is a contrast in fullness of detail—especially as it affects her young daughter. How Virginia herself was affected at the moment, she recalls in her *Diary* soon after the death of Roger Fry (Sept. 12, 1934): "Remember turning aside at mother's bed, when she had died and Stella took us in, to laugh, secretly, at the nurse crying. She's pretending, I said, aged 13, and was afraid I was not feeling enough. So now."

During these years just before and after the turn of the century, the young men of the family and their friends were

studying at Cambridge. Virginia, whose health did not permit of the conventional schooling, was educated at home,
learning among other things Greek with a teacher, Janet
Case, of whom she speaks in her *Diary* (July 19, 1937), after
Miss Case's death: "she was oddly inarticulate. No hand for
words. Her letters, save that the last began 'My beloved Virginia,' always cool and casual. And how I loved her, at Hyde
Park Gate: and how I went hot and cold going to Windmill
Hill: and how great a visionary part she has played in my life,
till the visionary became a part of the fictitious, not of the
real life." But she was not inarticulate when eleven years
earlier she had criticized *Mrs. Dalloway* as "all dressing...
technique"—a "damned criticism" that haunted Mrs. Woolf
(*Diary*, Sept. 13, 1926). She has much to say later about the
disparity in educational opportunity between the daughters
and the sons in educated families. Probably even in 1900
there was speculation in the eyes of the demure Victorian
girl having tea in her brother's rooms. And in *A Room of
One's Own* (1929) she expressed her mature convictions
about the education of women; and about life at Newnham
and Girton as compared with life at King's. But for all that,
she liked "those trusty Cambridge fellows," as she wrote in
her *Diary* when G. Lowes Dickinson died in 1932.

After Sir Leslie Stephen's death in 1904, Vanessa and Vir-
gina, Thoby and Adrian, lived together at 46 Gordon Square
—one of the Bloomsbury squares. Thoby died in 1906; Vanessa married Clive Bell in 1907, and the Bells took over the
Gordon Square house, Adrian and Virginia moving to nearby
Fitzroy Square. Between 1907 and 1912 Clive Bell was to
some extent Virginia's literary confidant (Clive Bell, *Old
Friends*). She had begun to write literary reviews in 1905,
when the connection with the *Times Literary Supplement*
(hereafter referred to as *TLS*), which lasted more than thirty
years, was established. She was closely associated with the
original Bloomsbury group, among whom was Lytton Stra-

chey, who had been Thoby's friend at Cambridge. On March 9, 1909, Lytton wrote to his brother James: "On Feb. 19th [a mistake for 17th] I proposed to Virginia and was accepted. It was an awkward moment, as you may imagine, especially as I realized the very minute it was happening, that the whole thing was repulsive to me. Her sense was amazing, and luckily it turned out that she's not in love. The result was that I was able to manage a fairly honourable retreat. . . . I need hardly mention the immense secrecy of the affair" (*Virginia Woolf and Lytton Strachey: Letters,* 1956). On the same day he wrote to her, "still rather agitated and exhausted." He hopes she is cheerful, but he is "all of a heap" and the future seems blank; "but whatever happens, as you said, the important thing is that we should like each other; and we can neither of us have any doubt that we do. This world is so difficult to manage." He was twenty-nine and she twenty-seven. This correspondence, according to the editors, Leonard Woolf and James Strachey, was rather sparse and spasmodic, and on neither side completely typical. They were wary of each other, a little self-conscious, and always on their best behavior. Of course they saw each other frequently. Many entries in the *Diary* are evidence of the deep respect Virginia Woolf had for his opinion of her work; and several of her essays on the art of biography contain interesting estimates of his achievements. But she did not review his books; the editor of the *TLS* did not approve of a friend reviewing a friend's work. The correspondence ends with Strachey's death in 1932.

Leonard Woolf had gone to Ceylon to take up a post in the Civil Service in 1904—the date at which the first volume of his autobiography, *Sowing,* ends. Not long after his return on leave, Virginia Stephen announced her engagement to him in a note to Strachey, June 6, 1912. They were married soon after. Some of the deepest interests that were to shape her work—she had at thirty published only book reviews—are very clear in retrospect. She was a Londoner born and bred, and London is seldom absent from her novels. Both *Mrs. Dalloway* and *The Years* are London books in more ways than one. Among the last entries in her *Diary* are expressions of grief and dismay over what was happening to her beloved city in the 1940 blitz. The summers spent in her childhood at St. Ives in Cornwall left sea memories that haunt her work; especially, of course, the sea novels, *The Waves* and *To the Lighthouse*. But even in the others there are sea images and rhythms and symbols. "The sea colors, green and blue, shine through her work" (Holtby, *Virginia Woolf*). The excitement of creation is associated with the sea. When she was beginning to imagine the book that became *Mrs. Dalloway*, she noted in her *Diary* (June 13, 1923), "Often now I have to control my excitement—as if I were pushing through a screen; or as if something beat fiercely close to me. . . . It is a general sense of the poetry of existence that overcomes me. Often it is connected with the sea and St. Ives." The city, the sea, and finally—books. The fascination reading held for her is beautifully expressed in a long essay, "Reading," posthumously published in *The Captain's Death Bed and Other Essays*. The setting is a library, but the essay no more records hours spent in any particular library on any one summer morning than "Street Haunting" records any particular long stroll through the streets of London on any one early winter evening. She had haunted libraries over the years as she had haunted streets, before she could write of the experience in a magical pattern of thought and imagery. There is no clue as to when she wrote "Reading." It was among the papers in a drawer where she put sketches and stories.

But this library—"I liked to read there." Summer, the windows open, a gardener mowing the lawn outside, flower beds and bees, and in perspective, tennis players. The reading was a part of the trees and the fields and the hot summer sky. Looking up from the page, the mind turned to the past,

and behind the voices heard, the figures seen from the window, stretched "an immeasurable avenue that ran to a point
of other voices, figures, fountains, which tapered out indis-
tinguishably upon the farthest horizon." And the books
seemed to go back to Keats, to Pope, and on to Chaucer.
"Even the gardener leading the pony was part of the book."
Such a man had changed little since Anglo-Saxon days, and
took his place naturally by the side of those dead poets. "He
ploughed; he sowed; he drank; he marched in battle sometimes; he sang his song; he came courting and went under-
ground, raising only a green wave in the turf of the church-
yard, but leaving boys and girls behind him to continue his
name and lead the pony across the lawn, these hot summer
mornings." The gardener suggests other figures in other layers
of time—knights and ladies, pictured in their repose in the
church, hands folded, eyes shut, favorite hounds at their feet.
One must see them, for one does not hear them—"the art of
speech came late to England." The reader thinks of the
Verneys and Pastons and Hutchinsons, who left treasures of
things curiously made and delicately figured, but only "a very
broken message." And she wonders, "Did they compose
themselves and cease their chatter when they sat down to
write what would pass from hand to hand, serve for winter
gossip round a dozen firesides and be laid up at length with
other documents of importance in the dry room above the
kitchen fireplace?" There was Lady Fanshawe, who bore
eighteen children in twenty-one years and buried most of
them; "writing is with them, as it can no longer be with us,
making; making something that will endure and wear a brave
face in the eyes of posterity." And the Leghs, generation after
generation, all red-haired, "all living at Lyme, which has been
building these three centuries and more, all men of education, character, and opportunity, and all, by modern standards, dumb." They will write of a fox hunt, but "having
killed their fox, drunk their punch, raced their horses, fought

their cocks, and toasted, discreetly, the King over the water . . . their lips shut, their eyes close; they have nothing more
to say to us." Dull they seem. But "if Lyme had been blotted
out and the thousand other houses of equal importance
which lay about England like little fortresses of civilization,
where you could read books, act plays, make laws, meet your
neighbours, and talk with strangers from abroad, if these
spaces won from the encroaching barbarity had not persisted
till the foothold was firm and the swamp withheld, how
would our more delicate spirits have fared—our writers, musi-
cians, artists—without a wall to shelter under, or flowers
upon which to sun their wings?" (In another essay, on Lady
Dorothy Nevill in *The Common Reader*, Mrs. Woolf has
other things to say about what sometimes went on in what
are "euphemistically" known as "the stately homes of England"—those "comfortably padded lunatic asylums.")

Going back through the long corridor of sunny mornings,
boring her way through hundreds of Augusts, the reader
comes to Queen Elizabeth, whom she evokes, flaunting across
the terrace superbly, Queen Elizabeth who "breakfasts off
beer and meat and handles the bones with fingers rough
with rubies," but who of all our kings and queens is most fit
for that gesture which bids the great sailors farewell or wel-
comes them home. And that brings to mind Hakluyt and the
ships and adventurers, and especially those who sailed far to
the north and were set down to wait in the white landscape
for the ships to appear the next summer. "Strange must have
been their thoughts; strange the sense of the unknown; and
of themselves, the isolated English, burning on the very rim
of the dark, and the dark full of unseen splendours." One of
them went inland to Moscow and saw the emperor "sitting in
his chair of estate, with his crown on his head and a staff of
goldsmith work in his left hand." [4]

4 Some of these phrases appear in "The Elizabethan Lumber
Room," *The Common Reader* I.

The lives of all these books filled the room with a soft murmur. "Truly, a deep sea the past, a tide which will overtake and overflow us." After a strange night excursion into the woods, trapping moths,[5] the reader comes back into the library in the morning hours, seeking something that has been shaped and clarified, "cut to catch the light, hard as gem or rock with the seal of human experience in it, and yet sheltering as in a clear gem the flame which burns now so high and now sinks so low in our own hearts." And so to poetry....

This free reverie in an ideal library expresses the delight in reading, the sense of the long past of English history, the sharp realization of the present moment—the inner and the outer streams mingling—and the continuing interplay of life and literature—all to be found in the disciplined critical writing of *The Common Reader*.

II

Two years after Virginia Woolf's marriage, the First World War broke out, ending that period of relative security and stability which all those, at least in the Western world, who grew up before 1914 look back upon with nostalgia. In 1940, in an address before the Workers' Educational Association at Brighton,[6] Mrs. Woolf risked the theory that peace and prosperity were influences that gave a family likeness to nineteenth-century writers, despite great individual differences. "They had leisure; they had security; life was not going to change; they themselves were not going to change. They

---

5 Vita Sackville-West, writing in *Encounter*, January, 1954, recalls asking Virginia Woolf why she was so much haunted by moths. She had written about the death of a moth; she had at first intended the title of *The Waves* to be *The Moths*. "Ah, that she could easily explain: in her youth she used to put grease-bands round the apple trees and go out with a torch and a jam-pot after dark."

6 Reprinted in *The Moment, and Other Essays*.

could look; and look away." Even as late as 1914 "we can still see the writer sitting as he sat all through the nineteenth century looking at human life; and that human life is still divided into classes; he still looks most intently at the class from which he himself springs; the classes are still so settled that he has almost forgotten that there are classes; and he is still so secure himself that he is almost unconscious of his own position and of its security. He believes that he is looking at the whole of life." She quotes Desmond MacCarthy, who began to write before 1914, on how the young men learned their art: "At College they say—by reading; by listening; by talking." At Cambridge, "we were not very much interested in politics. Abstract speculation was much more absorbing; philosophy was more interesting to us than public causes.... What we chiefly discussed were those 'goods' which were ends in themselves...the search for truth, aesthetic emotions, and personal relations." They read Latin and Greek, they traveled abroad, they rambled happily during long vacations through England, France, Italy; and now and then published books. "Then suddenly, like a chasm in a smooth road, the war came."

Desmond MacCarthy was one of the early Bloomsbury group, consisting of a "number of intimate friends who had been at Trinity and King's and were now working in London, most of them living in Bloomsbury" (L. Woolf, Sowing). Had it been a sort of exclusive club, it would be easier to draw up a list of members from the various sources.[7] They were friends, not members: the Stephens, the Bells, the Stracheys—Lytton, James, and Marjorie; Roger Fry, Duncan Grant, Leonard Woolf, Maynard Keynes; Sidney Saxon Turner—musician and civil servant; H. T. J. Norton—mathematician and don; and E. M. Forster; this does not exhaust

7 J. K. Johnstone, The Bloomsbury Group (1954); Leonard Woolf, Sowing (1960); Clive Bell, Old Friends (1956); TLS, Aug. 20, 1954; Noel Annan, Leslie Stephen (1951).

the list. After the war the circle was widened by younger people like Christopher Isherwood and David Garnett and others. Bloomsbury derived from Cambridge; that is, certain common values of the early group stemmed from the philosophy of the Cambridge philosopher G. E. Moore, as set forth in his *Principia Ethica* (1903). Moore was a Fellow of Trinity College when Leonard Woolf, Thoby Stephen, Clive Bell, and Lytton Strachey were undergraduates; and to judge from the section on Cambridge in *Sowing*, they had an intellectually exhilarating time, becoming accustomed to an atmosphere of intimate and free discussion that remained a tradition in the Bloomsbury group. Mr. Woolf recalls "the passionate distress which muddled thinking aroused" in Moore, his Socratic mind and method, the intensity of his passion for truth, and his simplicity and integrity. The values were moral and aesthetic, not religious; more concerned with being than doing; personal relationships were of the first importance. After the Cambridge undergraduates had been busy in the world for a while, the *Principia Ethica*, writes Leonard Woolf, "passed into our unconscious and was now merely a part of our super-ego; we no longer argued about it as a guide to practical life." Noel Annan, commenting on Moore's influence, writes, "With the help of G. E. Moore's philosophy they created an ethical justification for art for art's sake." They were much influenced by painting, by the ideas of Roger Fry and Clive Bell. The reviewer of *The Bloomsbury Group* (*TLS*, Aug. 20, 1954) makes the penetrating observation that it would have been a Bloomsbury heresy if, as artists, they had become aware that "rather than imposing pattern or significant form on a chaotic material universe, they were *discovering* it there." To an outsider, he adds, this appears to be just what Virginia Woolf was doing. And he quotes E. M. Forster's slightly heretical remark, "Perhaps life is a mystery and not a muddle."

Christopher Isherwood wrote in *Decision* (1941) that the

Bloomsbury group were "held together by consanguinity of talent" and that "artistic integrity was the family religion." Yet there was something very irritating about Bloomsbury, and Bloomsbury-baiters are not extinct. One reason for the irritation is suggested in the *TLS* review of Virginia Woolf's *Granite and Rainbow* (July 4, 1958): the Bloomsbury group, earlier and later, "avoided bores as far as possible, disliked pretences, and felt a marked partiality for their friends.... The spectacle of gifted people enjoying themselves is never one to give pleasure to the onlooker." Virginia Woolf's gifts were certainly enhanced by the company she kept. "She throve on discusssion," and if she was among the leaders of that company, "she also needed to whet her intuitions against the criticism of others." The English novelist Angus Wilson recalled in the *New York Times Book Review* (July 2, 1961) that his first postwar broadcast was an attack on Virginia Woolf, whose books had nurtured him as an adolescent and against whose influence he was reacting. He had attacked her "feminine hypersensitivity" and overconcern with personal values, "which I attributed to a private income and a long tradition of upper-middle-class security." Today, he added, he would hesitate to attack Virginia Woolf and the Bloomsbury school at all.

III

The Hogarth Press was started in 1917 by Mr. and Mrs. Woolf as a "hobby of printing rather than publishing." [8] The first publication, printed by the authors on a hand press, was *Two Stories*—Virginia Woolf's *The Mark on the Wall* and Leonard Woolf's *Three Jews*—in July, 1917. From 1915 to 1924 they were living at Hogarth House, Richmond.[9] They

8 See B. J. Kirkpatrick, A *Bibliography of Virginia Woolf* (1957).
9 Richmond Park is well stocked with deer. Winifred Holtby (*Virginia Woolf*) notes that after the Richmond period stags appear in Mrs. Woolf's works.

also had a lease of Asheham House near Lewes in Sussex, where they spent weekends and holidays, until in 1919 they bought Monks House, Rodmell, near Lewes. From 1924 until August, 1939, their London home, and the home of the Press, was at 52 Tavistock Square in Bloomsbury.

During these years, while her reputation as a writer was slowly growing, Virginia Woolf's life was filled with her writing, the activities of the Hogarth Press, holidays abroad and in England, occasional illnesses,[10] and the many interests of her family and her friends. For a vivid impression of what her daily life was like we can turn to the correspondence with Vita Sackville-West, extensively quoted by Aileen Pippett in *The Moth and the Star* and covering the period from 1922 to 1941. *A Writer's Diary* contains selections made by Leonard Woolf from the twenty-six volumes of the diary which she kept from 1915 until four days before her death. In his preface to the book Mr. Woolf states that he extracted and published "practically everything which referred to her own writing." He also included passages in which she was practicing or trying out her art; other passages that give an idea of "the direct impact upon her mind of scenes and persons," and passages of comment upon the books she was reading. Clive Bell (*Old Friends*) thinks that what we have of the diary in this selection gives a one-sided impression, concerned as it is so much with the anguish of writing, the anxiety about the opinions of her friends and the public, and her self-doubt. She herself noted (Feb. 28, 1939): "It is unfortunate for truth's sake that I never write here except when jangled with talk. I only record the dumps and the dismals and them very barely." Actually, according to Mr. Bell, she was about the gayest human being he had known and her talk was "dazzling"; that "enchanting soliloquy," *The Mark on the Wall*, gives a hint of what it was like when in conversation she indulged in a flight of fancy; and "Or-

10 See "On Being Ill," in *The Moment, and Other Essays.*

lando gives the best idea of her with her elbows on the tea-table letting herself go." Mr. Bell, who has seen unpublished parts of the diary, comments on references to still living people, which sometimes show that she experienced life as a novel in which her friends, all unknowing, might be cast for a part. He gives examples from his own memory.

Christopher Isherwood's first impression of Mrs. Woolf was of an "unhappy high-born lady in a ballad, a fairy-tale princess under a spell," with "wonderful forlorn eyes" (*Decision*, 1941). But he goes on, "What rubbish! We are at the tea-table, Virginia is sparkling with gaiety, delicate malice and gossip—the gossip which is the style of her books and which made her the best hostess in London." David Garnett, who came to know her well during the years of the war, also describes her in company: "Virginia, holding a cigarette, would lean forward before speaking and clear her throat with a motion like that of a noble bird of prey, then, as she spoke, excitement would suddenly come as she visualised what she was saying and her voice would crack, like a schoolboy's, on a higher note. And in that cracked high note one felt all her humour and delight in life. Then she would throw herself back in her chair with a hoot of laughter, intensely amused by her own words." When she came over from Asheham, "she brought the wind off the Downs into the house with her, she had a warmth and good-fellowship which set people at their ease. . . . Her voice and her glance were filled with affection, mockery, curiosity, comradeship." She was a wonderful raconteur—"she saw everyone, herself included, with detachment, and life itself as a vast Shakespearean comedy. She loved telling stories at her own expense—some of them as ribald as anything in Chaucer—for all her personal vanity was forgotten in the storyteller's art." [11]

The farmhouse at Asheham, as Mr. Garnett describes it, looked across the valley of the Ouse to Rodmell. It had dou-

[11] David Garnett, *The Flowers of the Forest* (1955), pp. 160–61.

ble French windows with arched lights over them, giving the façade "a curiously dream-like character," and it was supposed to be haunted. Although he himself never saw a ghost, Mr. Garnett says that Clive Bell did—a figure passing from room to room and crossing the windows. Virginia Woolf's "lovely sketch," *A Haunted House*, evokes the ghost of Asheham, "a house with a personal character as individual as that of a woman one has loved, and who is dead." "Places explain people," he goes on. "They become impregnated with the spirit of those who have lived and been happy in them. For a full understanding of Virginia, who spent her holidays and week-ends there for several years after her marriage, Asheham would greatly help. But the clue is almost gone—it is more a memory than a reality and in common with all the houses which Virginia made her own, there was suggestion in it of a timeless, underwater world." [12]

There is an odd resemblance between this suggestion and that of Winifred Holtby, in her description of the study in Tavistock Square—an immense half-subterranean room, piled with books; "there one seems to move among books and papers as among the rocks and ledges of that submarine cave of which the characters in her books are always dreaming. The light penetrates wanly down between the high buildings overhead, as through deep waters, and noises from the outside world enter only in a subdued murmur, as from very far away." [13]

Mrs. Woolf, like her Bloomsbury friends, could be irritating, and she could even irritate those within her circle, like E. M. Forster, who found one side of her "very peculiar"— her feminism. Three of her books—*Orlando*, *A Room of One's Own*, and *Three Guineas*—deal with the subject, and many of her book reviews and essays and passages in her *Diary* express feminist attitudes. The "present time" with

12 *Ibid.*, pp. 102 f.
13 Holtby, *Virginia Woolf*, p. 35.

Brigid Brophy: " An instance of a novel
more factitious than fictitious ... "

which *Orlando* ends, October, 1928, was the month in which she gave the lectures at Newnham and Girton on "Women and Fiction," later altered and expanded into A *Room of One's Own*. Within its informal framework old questions are freshly examined; as, for instance, are women inferior, if they are, to men in literature and the arts, because of congenital deficiency, or because of circumstances—political, economic, religious, and social conditions at different periods in different societies? What might have happened to a possible sister of Shakespeare, endowed with a quick fancy and a lively imagination and an adventurous spirit? "But she was not sent to school. She had no chance of learning grammar and logic, let alone of reading Horace and Virgil. She picked up a book now and then, one of her brother's perhaps, and read a few pages. But then her parents came in and told her to mend the stockings or mind the stew and not moon about with books and papers." Pursuing this fancy, Mrs. Woolf pictures how she would be betrothed, how kind her parents would be in planning the best for a daughter in that society, but how she wanted to act and ran away to London and was laughed at, for no woman could be an actress. And how in the end she was seduced and killed herself one winter's night and "lies buried at some cross-roads where the omnibuses now stop outside the Elephant and Castle." This intriguing speculation is followed by another perhaps better grounded. When one reads of "a witch being ducked, of a woman possessed by devils, of a wise woman selling herbs, or even of a very remarkable man who had a mother, then I think we are on the track of a lost novelist, a suppressed poet, of some mute and inglorious Jane Austen, some Emily Brontë who dashed her brains out on the moor or mopped and mowed about the highways crazed with the torture her gift had put her to." And what about Anon, who wrote so many poems without signing them? Maybe sometimes that was a woman; certainly no one can disprove it.

× Brigid Brophy: " It is a sterile book; a whimsical, frequently facetious panoramic stroll through English history and literature."

Outside the creative mood, as Joan Bennett points out,[14] Mrs. Woolf believed in woman suffrage, but the characters in her novels who are involved in the movement are treated with a mixture of sympathy and irony, from Evelyn in *The Voyage Out*, who plans to form a club to discuss things that "really matter to people's lives—the White Slave Traffic, Woman Suffrage," to Rose Pargiter of *The Years*, who goes to jail for the Cause and is forcibly fed. But it is not the vote for women that concerns Mrs. Woolf in *A Room of One's Own* but opportunities for women—to have their own economic rooms, to be as well educated as their brothers, and not to be warned off the grass by the beadles of the universities. For even in the first quarter of the twentieth century, in a great university like Cambridge, women had a precarious foothold, won at the cost of great sacrifices, and their way of life at Newnham was meager compared to that of their brothers at King's. The contrast is humorously pointed up by what E. M. Forster described as the "exquisite" lunch with the dons at King's and the "deplorable" dinner the same evening with the ladies at Newnham. Searching through the catalogue of the British Museum for light upon what men have thought about Woman during the centuries, Mrs. Woolf is led far afield to witty and thought-provoking reflections upon such topics as the contrast—in training for a novelist—between Charlotte Brontë's restricted experience and Tolstoy's wide-ranging adventures; friendships between women as a theme for fiction; and the androgynous mind of the artist.

Nine years later, *Three Guineas* relies on documentation to prove its points. Entries in the *Diary* from 1931 on show how seriously Mrs. Woolf was taking the obligation to express the feminist viewpoint. She felt justified in writing the book, because editors were always asking her opinion on all sorts of subjects, from short skirts and smoking to war; and

14 *Virginia Woolf*, pp. 76 f.

she first thought of writing a sequel to *A Room of One's Own.* Then she was irritated by H. G. Wells on Woman— "how she must be ancillary and decorative in the world of the future, because she has been tried, in ten years, and has not proved anything" (Feb. 11, 1932).[15] And one morning (April 9, 1935) she happened to meet her friend E. M. Forster in the London Library, and he told her there had been a discussion whether to allow ladies on the committee; and recalled that Sir Leslie Stephen had found a certain Mrs. Green years ago very troublesome. This made her so angry that her hand trembled, and she decided to entitle her book *On Being Despised.* As the threat of war grew, so did the urgent need to write about the causes and prevention of war. She was asked to contribute to groups and societies connected directly or indirectly with the problem. How apportion her three guineas? So the book grew into a long pamphlet, and its publication aroused both anger and admiration. She notes (June 3, 1938) that the *TLS* called her the "most brilliant pamphleteer in England." Q. V. Leavis attacked her violently in *Scrutiny;* E. M. Forster thought the arguments outdated. A letter to V. Sackville-West is quoted by Aileen Pippett: "Of course I knew you wouldn't like 3 gns. That's why I wouldn't, unless you had sent me a postcard with a question, have given it you. You say you don't agree with 50% of it. No, of course you don't. . . . It may be a silly book—I don't agree that it's a well-written book, but it's certainly an honest book; and I took more pains to get up the facts and state them plainly than I ever took with anything in my life. . . . All I wanted was to state a very intricate case as plainly and reasonably as I could." [16]

From a lengthening perspective, including the war that was not prevented, Bernard Blackstone, writing in 1949, calls

15 In 1919 an act was passed unbarring the professions to women (*Three Guineas,* p. 30).
16 *The Moth and the Star,* p. 303.

Three Guineas a somber book and in its way a great book, full of a massive integrity. She faces the horror of war—at that moment the prelude in Spain, the conflict in which her nephew Julian Bell was killed—and "sets her frail but stead-fast vision of reality against the lie of society." [17]

In an article in the *Forum* (1929) she asks why there was no continuous writing done by women before the eighteenth century. From Sappho on there were strange intermissions of silence and speech. The answer, she suggests, lies locked in old diaries, stuffed away in old drawers, in the "lives of the obscure... in those almost unlit corridors of history, where the figures of generations of women are so dimly, so fitfully perceived." The history of England is the history of the male line. Only when the conditions of the average woman's life are known can we account for the success or failure of the extraordinary woman as a writer. She had occasion to say something about the conditions of workingwomen in England about 1913 when an officer of the Women's Cooperative Guild turned over to her some papers about their lives written by workingwomen, members of the Guild. They were to be used in a book, *Life as We Have Known It*, with an introduction by Virginia Woolf.[18] In 1913 she had attended a meeting of the Guild and listened to the speeches of the delegates, demanding shorter hours and higher wages, sanitation and education; and she tries after seventeen years to recapture some of her impressions of that meeting. Like most of the middle-class audience from London, she was a benevolent spectator, but one who imagined what it would be like to be Mrs. Giles of Durham or Mrs. Edwards of Wolverton. "But, after all, the imagination is largely a child of the flesh. One could not be Mrs. Giles because one's body had never stood at the wash tub; one's hands had never

17 *Virginia Woolf, A Commentary.*
18 Published by the Hogarth Press, 1931. Reprinted in *The Captain's Death Bed, and Other Essays.*

wrung and scrubbed and chopped up whatever the meat may
be that makes a miner's dinner." Irrelevancies were always
coming into the picture. "One saw landscapes or seascapes,
in Greece or perhaps in Italy, where Mrs. Giles or Mrs.
Edwards must have seen slag heaps and row upon row of
slate roofs in a mining village." Such things creeping in from
another world falsified the picture and made the game too
much of a game to be worth playing. So having, like Jane
Austen, a saving perception of her own limitations, she did
not try in her fiction to do what she couldn't do. But she
did try to understand that the working classes, far from being downtrodden, envious, and exhausted, were "humorous,
vigorous and thoroughly independent." If one could meet
them, not as sympathizers, or masters and mistresses, but
casually as fellow beings, "a great liberation would follow."
Think of the words that must lurk in their vocabulary that
have faded out of ours; of the images and proverbial sayings
still current; of the scenes "that lie dormant in their eyes
unseen by us." But, sticking up for her class, she remarks
that "no working man or woman works harder with his hands
or is in closer touch with reality than a painter with his
brush or a writer with his pen." And her class has as much to
give them as theirs has to give hers—"wit and detachment,
learning and poetry and all those good gifts which those who
have never answered bells or touched their foreheads with
their forefingers enjoy by right." This sounds rather quaint
thirty years later in a changed England, and would certainly
ruffle the feathers of such angry young men as the reviewer
of Mrs. Woolf's *Diary*, who labels her arrogant with "the
arrogance of the aesthete—as horrible and intolerant as the
arrogance of wealth." [19] But for all that she sees the meaning of these lives she read. "So it was that in the year 1913
Mrs. Robson and Mrs. Potter and Mrs. Wright were getting
up and asking not only for baths and wages and electric light,

19 *Adelphi*, Vol. XXX, 1954.

but also for cooperative industry and adult suffrage and the
taxation of land values and divorce law reform. It was thus
that they were to ask, as the years went by, for peace and
disarmament and the sisterhood of nations. And the force
that lay behind their speeches was compact of many things—
of men with whips, and sick rooms where match boxes were
made, of hunger and cold, and many and difficult childbirths,
of much scrubbing and washing up, or reading Shelley and
William Morris and Samuel Butler, of meetings of the
Women's Guild and committees and congresses at Man-
chester and elsewhere."

Writing to V. Sackville-West (1926), she describes a
meeting at which the Countess Tatiana Tolstoy lectured to
a Mayfair audience of ladies who had sables on their backs,
whose cheeks seemed made of pâté de fois gras, and who
had "nothing left of humanity or emotion at all." Said Tatiana, "The ladies will know what it means to nurse thirteen
children." Mrs. Woolf "hated us all for being prosperous and
comfortable and wished to be a working woman and wished
to be able to excuse my life to Tolstoy." At this time there
was great economic distress. South Wales was a "devastated
area, the Clyde shipyards were deserted, steel furnaces cold
and mills silent in county after county and mournful hunger
marchers converged on London without ever disturbing the
complacency of Berkeley Square." [20] One remembers that
Elizabeth Dalloway hears the bands of hunger marchers
when she ventures alone along the Strand, and these sounds
are to be heard also in *The Years*. Mrs. Woolf went with
her husband to Labour party conferences, but "in public
she took little part in discussions; in private she supported
her husband." [21] At one Labour party meeting at Brighton
(*Diary*, Oct. 2, 1935), she was moved by a speech by George
Lansbury and worried if her duty as a human being required

20 Pippett, *The Moth and the Star*, pp. 217–18.
21 *Ibid.*, p. 304.

C

her to work at altering the structure of society—"but when is it altered?" The women delegates were "very thin-voiced and unsubstantial. On Monday one said it is time we gave up washing up. A thin frail protest but genuine. A little reed piping, but what chance against all this weight of roast beef and beer—which she must cook." A little earlier (Feb. 26, 1935) she was "plagued by the sudden wish to write an anti-Fascist pamphlet." By the next spring Hitler's army was on the Rhine, and the guns were near their private lives again, but "I go on like a doomed mouse, nibbling at my daily page." Aldous Huxley had refused to sign some manifesto because it approved sanctions and he was a pacifist. "So am I. Ought I to resign. L. says that considering Europe is now on the verge of the greatest smash for 600 years, one must sink private differences and support the League" (*Diary*, March 13, 1936). In December she wrote one article in the Communist *Daily Worker*—"Why Art Follows Politics." [22] By the following spring the refugees from the war in Spain were invading Bloomsbury. She saw a procession of children, women, young men, as she approached Tavistock Square—"a shuffling trudging procession, flying—impelled by machine gun in Spanish fields to trudge through Tavistock Square, along Gordon Square, then where?—clasping their enamel kettles." This long trail of fugitives—"like a caravan in a desert"—brought tears to her eyes, "though no one seemed surprised" (June 23, 1937).

At the time of the Munich crisis she was working on her biography of Roger Fry, thinking of 1910 and Gordon Square, and the crisis seemed unreal: "All these grim men

22 Reprinted in *The Moment, and Other Essays*. Perhaps this one aberration was enough to assure her of a place on the list of 2,300 English people, drawn up by Herr Himmler, marked for immediate incarceration upon the successful invasion of Britain. Her friends E. M. Forster and Bertrand Russell are included—along with Winston Churchill, Bernard Shaw, and a distinguished assortment of *Who's Who* (see Shirer, *Rise and Fall of the Third Reich*, p. 784, fn.).

appear to me like grown-ups staring incredulously at a child's sand castle which for some inexplicable reason has become a real vast castle, needing gunpowder and dynamite to destroy it. Nobody in their senses can believe it, yet nobody must tell the truth" (*Diary*, Sept. 10, 1938).

IV

The war came, and as in 1914, opened a chasm in the road, though scarcely without warning. The *Diary* entries were divided between London and Rodmell. From Rodmell Mrs. Woolf wrote on September 6, 1939, "our first air raid warning at 8:30 this morning. . . . Boredom. All meaning has run out of everything. . . . My plan is to force my brain to work on Roger [*Roger Fry: A Biography*]. . . . Endless interruptions. . . . We have carried coals etc. into the cottage for the Battersea women and children. The expectant mothers are all quarreling. Some went back yesterday. . . . Going to London tomorrow I expect frightens me. . . . This war has begun in cold blood. One merely feels that the killing machine has to be set in action. So far, the *Athenia* has been sunk. . . . Perfect summer weather." The London address after August was 37 Mecklenburgh Square. "The break in our lives from London to country is a far more complete one than any change of house. . . . Odd how often I think with what is love I suppose of the City" (Feb. 2, 1940). She kept at work on the biography—a steady grind, relieved by the growing conception of the "fantastic" *Poyntz Hall,* which became *Between the Acts,* and by book reviews (chiefly for the *New Statesman and Nation*); and of course by her reading. Freud gave her an insight into the writings of the Leaning Tower group, the young men of the thirties, whose tower of class security had begun to lean perilously, and who, unable to describe society, described themselves—in a sort of autoanalysis—as the products or victims; "a necessary step towards freeing the next generation of repressions." [23]

From May, 1940, anxiety mounted through the months of threatened invasion. May 13, 1940: "We're in the third day of 'the greatest battle in history.'" The wireless announced the fall of Holland and Belgium. "Duncan saw an air battle over Charleston—a silver pencil and a puff of smoke.... But though L. says he has petrol in the garage for suicide should Hitler win, we go on." May 25: "Rodmell burns with rumours. Are we to be bombed, evacuated? Guns that shake the windows." A hospital train passes through the green fields, there are wild duck flights of aeroplanes overhead. A wounded German plane dipped among the fir trees and did not rise. September 18, 1940: "'We have need of all our courage' are the words that come to the surface this morning: on hearing that all our windows are broken, ceilings down, and most of our china smashed at Mecklenburgh Square.... The Press—what remains—is to be moved to Letchworth. A grim morning." October 12: "In London, now, or two years ago, I'd be owling through the streets.... I imagine a village invasion. Queer the contraction of life to the village radius. Wood bought enough to stack many winters. All our friends are isolated over winter fires. Chance of interruption small now. No cars. No petrol. Trains uncertain. And we on our lovely free autumn island. But I will read Dante, and for my trip through the English literature book." On October 20, after a visit to London, she described the heap of ruins at 32 Tavistock Square: "I could just see a piece of my studio wall standing: otherwise rubble where I wrote so many books. Open air where we sat so many nights, gave so many parties.... Exhilaration at losing possessions—save at times I want

23 *Diary*, Feb. 11, 1940. See "The Leaning Tower," *Folios of New Writing*, Autumn, 1940. Mrs. Woolf had read a paper the preceding spring before the Workers' Educational Association at Brighton. Reprinted in *The Moment*.

my books and chairs and carpets and beds. How I worked to buy them—one by one—and the pictures." John Lehmann recalls in an article in the *Listener* (Jan. 13, 1955), "Working with Virginia Woolf," the rooms at the top of the Tavistock Square house, "rooms fabulous for me on account of their wall paintings by Duncan Grant and Vanessa Bell—paintings so strangely exposed to the public gaze when a nazi bomb ripped through the house." January 15, 1941: "We were in London on Monday. I went to London Bridge. I looked at the river; very misty; some tufts of smoke, perhaps from burning houses.... So by Tube to the Temple; and there wandered in the desolate ruins of my old squares: gashed; dismantled; the old red bricks all white powder, something like a builder's yard. Grey dirt and broken windows. Sightseers; all that completeness ravished and demolished."

"The Germans were over this house last night and the night before that. Here they are again. It is a queer experience, lying in the dark and listening to the zoom of a hornet which may at any moment sting you to death. It is a sound that interrupts cool and consecutive thinking about peace. Yet it is a sound ... that should compel one to think about peace. Unless we can think peace into existence we—not this one body in this one bed but millions of bodies yet to be born—will lie in the same darkness and hear the same death rattle overhead." So begins "Thoughts on Peace in an Air Raid," an article contributed by Mrs. Woolf to a symposium in the *New Republic*, October 21, 1940.[24] The tone is adapted to an American audience, not yet concerned about air raids. Another hornet had zoomed in *The Times* that morning—the voice of Lady Astor, complaining that women had no voice in politics and that all the idea-makers in a position to make ideas effective were men. This sounds rather like the Virginia Woolf of *Three Guineas*. But this Virginia

24 Reprinted in *The Death of the Moth*.

Woolf of 1940, lying in the dark with a gas mask handy, reflects: "Are we not stressing our disability because our disability exposes us perhaps to abuse, perhaps to contempt? 'I will not cease from mental fight,' Blake wrote. Mental fight means thinking against the current, not with it." There is a spate of words about free people fighting to defend freedom. Who is free? The young airman circling among the clouds is no more free than the woman lying in bed, listening in the dark—both prisoners, "he boxed up in his machine with a gun handy; we lying in the dark with a gas mask handy." What is involved in the fight for real freedom, she can only suggest in a short article; and she concludes with a message to the men and women in America, whose sleep had not yet been broken by machine-gun fire, in the hope that these fragmentary notes will be shaped by them into something serviceable. "And now, in the shadowed half of the world, to sleep."

They slept with gas masks handy at Rodmell, but the Indian summer days were beautiful. "Ought I not to look at the sunset rather than write this? A flush of red in the blue; the haystack on the marsh catches the glow; behind me, the apples are red in the trees." A solemn stillness in the air until 8:30, "when the cadaverous twanging in the sky begins; the planes going to London." The bombs which were dropped, aimed at the power works, fell closer every time. "Caburn was crowned with what looked like a settled moth, wings extended—a Messerschmitt it was, shot down on Sunday" (*Diary*, Oct. 2, 1940). In November the river burst its banks and the marsh became a "sea with gulls on it." The flood increased with the tremendous rain and marsh walks became impossible. But it was beautiful; "incredible beauty" of the haystack in the marsh water, "in the sun deep blue"— an inland sea. When the floods subsided in December, she could ride across the downs to the cliffs. In January there was frost, still frost, burning white, burning blue. "And I can't help even now turning to look at Asheham down, red, purple, dove blue grey, with the cross so melodramatically against it."

There are ominous references in January and February to "a battle against depression." But she is determined not to be engulfed in the "trough of despair." She continued to make plans for new books, for reading; she visited Newnham, and went to Brighton for a meeting at which her husband spoke. There was a lull in the war in January: "Six nights without raids. But Garvin says the greatest struggle is about to come —say in three weeks—and every man, woman, dog, cat, even weevil must girt their arms, their faith—and so on. It's the cold hour, this: before the lights go up. A few snowdrops in the garden. Yes, I was thinking: we live without a future. That's what's queer: with our noses pressed to a closed door." [25]

The strains to which Mrs. Woolf was subjected, whatever interpretation has been placed upon them, proved too great. When on March 28, 1941, she disappeared, she opened that closed door and sought death in the river near her home, leaving her hat and walking stick on the bank.

25 *Diary,* Jan. 26, 1941.

Brigid Brophy: " Virginia Woolf's novels are too devastatingly vague."

2. Criticism

The Uncommon Reader as Critic

I

AFTER WRITING book reviews for twenty years, Virginia Woolf prepared her first collection of literary essays entitled *The Common Reader*. She took her title from Dr. Johnson, who in his *Life of Gray* rejoiced "to concur with the common reader; for by the common sense of readers, uncorrupted by literary prejudices, after all the refinements of subtilty and the dogmatism of learning, must be generally decided all claim to poetical honours." Describing this common reader, Mrs. Woolf declared him to be worse educated than the critic and the scholar; reading for his own pleasure "rather than to impart knowledge or correct the opinions of others ... guided by an instinct to create for himself, out of whatever odds and ends he can come by, some kind of whole— a portrait of a man, a sketch of an age, a theory of the art of writing.... Hasty, inaccurate, and superficial, snatching now this poem, now that scrap of old furniture without caring where he finds it or of what nature it may be so long as it serves his purpose and rounds his structure, his deficiencies as a critic are too obvious to be pointed out." But if Dr. Johnson is right, he may have some say in "the final distribution of poetical honours." Dr. Johnson did not imply that he himself was a "common reader"—he only maintained that

32

the common sense of readers was decisive in the final awarding of honors. But Mrs. Woolf called herself a common reader, reading for her own pleasure and writing about what she read, yet knowing perfectly well that she was quite as "uncommon" in the art of reading as Dr. Johnson.

In an address on professions for women Mrs. Woolf once gave a somewhat fanciful account of how a young woman, with a room of her own, took up her pen one day, wrote something and mailed it to an editor and received a check for one pound ten and six, and bought a Persian cat with it.[1] The first review identified in the *Bibliography* as by Mrs. Woolf appeared in the *TLS* of March 10, 1905; in 1908 there were thirteen in the *TLS* and six in the *Cornhill Magazine*; and in 1918, forty-three in the *TLS*—reviews of essays, novels, letters, poetry, criticism, Russian fiction, by an impressive list of authors, including Conrad, Hugh Walpole, Wells, Hudson, Coleridge, Swinburne, Whitman, Compton Mackenzie, Rupert Brooke, Siegfried Sassoon, Aldous Huxley, Chekhov, Pepys, Edith Sitwell, and A.E. In 1938 Bruce Richmond, the editor of the *TLS* from 1902 to 1937, wrote Mrs. Woolf a grateful letter, ending a connection of more than thirty years, during which she had received "almost weekly orders." "How pleased I used to be when L. called me 'You're wanted by the Major Journal!'... I learnt a lot of my craft writing for him: how to compress; how to enliven; and also was made to read with a pen and notebook, seriously" (*Diary*, May 27, 1938). T. S. Eliot wrote an article in the *TLS*, January 13, 1961, in celebration of the ninetieth birthday of Bruce Lyttelton Richmond, for whom he began to review about 1920. To be invited to write for the *TLS*, said Mr. Eliot, was "to have reached the top rung of the ladder of literary journalism"—he was overawed. One of the reasons, surely, for the reputation that overawed Mr. Eliot was the distinction of the

1 "Professions for Women," in *The Death of the Moth, and Other Essays.*

anonymous contributions by Virginia Woolf. Anonymity imposed a discipline that Mr. Eliot considered a valuable experience for any young literary critic: "I learnt to moderate
my dislikes and crotchets, to write in a temperate and impartial way; I learnt that some things are permissible when they
appear over one's own name, which become tasteless eccen-
tricity or unseemly violence when unsigned." The writer must
submit himself to the editor, but the editor must be a man
to whom he can submit himself and preserve his self-respect.
"Bruce Richmond was a great editor."

Of the 291 reviews listed in the *Bibliography* as by Virginia
Woolf, 219 appeared in the *TLS*; 209 reviews have not so far
been reprinted, in either *The Common Reader* I and II or
the posthumous volumes of essays. Among these 209 there
are rewards for the searcher in the back files of the *TLS* and
other periodicals; but many are notices of books of ephemeral
interest, which fall into the class of "the stuffed books which
will come to pieces when they have lain about for a year or
two." [2] Mrs. Woolf's signed reviews appeared in *Cornhill
Magazine, National Review, Athenaeum, New Statesman,
New Statesman and Nation, London Mercury, Criterion,
Time and Tide, Nation and Athenaeum, Life and Letters,
Fortnightly Review, Listener, Folios of New Writing*; and in
the United States, *New Republic, Atlantic Monthly, Yale
Review, Harper's Bazaar, Bookman, Forum, New York Her-
ald Tribune Books, Saturday Review of Literature, Broom,
Dial, Vogue,* and *Living Age.* [3]

Mrs. Woolf was neither a literary nor an academic critic
in the sense defined by Angus Wilson in a review of *The
Garnett Family,* by Carolyn Heilbrun, in the *Listener* (Aug.
3, 1961): "It is probable that this decade will see the end
of private scholarship and of literary critics who are not
qualified by holding university appointments." She did not

2 "Hours in a Library," in *Granite and Rainbow.*
3 See *A Bibliography of Virginia Woolf.*

hold a chair in a college. Many of her literary essays grew out
of the request by an editor to review a book or commemo-
rate an anniversary; thus many of her choices of subject were
thrust upon her. Independent critical projects of her own
were often—on the evidence of the *Diary*—pushed aside by
the demands of her fiction. It is therefore rather out of order
to criticize her (as Mr. Leavis does in *The Great Tradition*)
for not making, "in a characteristic and not very satisfactory
essay on George Eliot," a serious attempt at revising the
judgment on *Middlemarch*. When she described *Middlemarch* as "one of the few English novels written for grown-up
people"—an opinion Mr. Leavis considers had a good deal to
do with the established recognition of *Middlemarch*—she was
really writing about the position of women in Victorian England and examining George Eliot's heroines as incomplete
versions of George Eliot's own story. They might have been
more satisfactory heroines if George Eliot had not, through
them, been reaching out for "all that life could offer the free
and inquiring mind" and confronting her feminine aspirations with the real world of men.[4] The book to be reviewed
often defines the problem to be discussed in Mrs. Woolf's
critical essays, which are "only rarely criticism in the strict
academic sense, but are frequently history, biography, discourse or argument." [5] Mrs. Woolf did not think too highly
of what was going on in the universities where, by 1930, the
arts of reading and writing were being extensively taught,
where degrees were given for "proficiency in one's native
tongue," and where "erudite and eugenic offspring" were being produced who knew the whole course of English literature, and how one age follows another, and one influence
cancels another, and one phrase is better than another; and
what with tutors and lecturers and examiners, the years of

4 See "George Eliot," *The Common Reader* I.
5 David Daiches, *Virginia Woolf*, 1945, p. 140. Section C of the
invaluable *Bibliography* gives the titles of the books reviewed.

falling in love with words were supervised.[6] Mrs. Woolf did
not live to see how the erudite offspring in their turn have
produced the critics who hold university appointments, have
disciples, and have ended, in Mr. Wilson's phrase, the criticism of private scholarship. She probably would have been
unhappy at these developments. But one might have pointed
out to her that her initiation into literature in her father's
library and among his friends and her Cambridge brothers
and their friends; and later her freedom to write as she
pleased in a room of her own; and to converse with artists
and writers and intellectuals of all sorts, old and young, in
Gordon Square and Fitzroy Square and all the Bloomsbury
squares; and to have a Press in the family basement and
manuscripts coming in from young writers to be rejected or
published—all that fostering of the critical sense, and that
superb reading background and living discussion, constituted
a training that could scarcely fall to anyone's lot nowadays.

Reading the *Diary* notes on the talk that went on through
the years during weekends, at teas and dinners and parties in
the country and in town, makes one wonder that she had
time to write. She visits Hardy in Dorset at teatime, "a little
puffy-cheeked cheerful old man," who talked of her father,
and of his own books, and of H. G. Wells and E. M. Forster
and Siegfried Sassoon (1926). They dined with the Webbs,
and she had some friendly easy talk with Hugh Macmillan
about the Buchans, and the Webbs were friendly—"but can't
be influenced about Kenya" (1929). "Lytton lunched here
on Saturday with the Webbs, and when I told him my various triumphs, did I imagine a little shade, instantly dispelled,
but not before my rosy fruit was out of the sun. Well, I
treated his triumphs in much the same way.... We ate in the
garden and Lytton sported very gracefully" (1919). Max
Beerbohm—"like a Cheshire cat. Orbicular. Jowled. Blue-

---

6 "All About Books," *New Statesman and Nation*, Feb. 28, 1931.
Reprinted in *The Captain's Death Bed*.

eyed"—rattled off opinions and reminiscences about Roger Fry and George Moore and Strachey—who said to him, "first I write one sentence; then I write another. That's how I write. And so I go on. But I have a feeling writing ought to be like running through a field. That's your way.... What you said in your beautiful essay about me and Charles Lamb was quite true" (1938). In 1933, walking down to the Serpentine on a summer evening, they met Shaw—"dwindled shanks, white beard"—striding along, and they talked for fifteen minutes; "a great spurt of ideas"—he had recently returned from China. "He stood with his arms folded, very upright" and broke off his monologue with "What a nice little dog. But aren't I keeping you and making you cold? (touching my arm)." On a wet Bank Holiday in 1934, she had tea with Maynard Keynes, who had had teeth out, "but was very fertile" on the subject of German politics and finance. After Arnold Bennett died in 1930, Mrs. Woolf recalled that she had talked with him at a party, or rather he talked, about George Moore and Desmond MacCarthy and Arnold Bennett, until she drew Lord David Cecil into the conversation. "And we taunted the old creature with thinking us refined. He said the gates of Hatfield were shut— 'shut away from life.' 'But open on Thursdays,' said Lord D. 'I don't want to go on Thursdays,' said B. 'And you drop your aitches on purpose,' I said, 'thinking that you possess more *life* than we do.' 'I sometimes tease,' said B., 'but I don't think I possess more life than you do.' " Even when she was most absorbed in *The Waves* she never stopped seeing people; perhaps when she was lying on the sofa between tea and dinner—friends like Rose Macaulay and Elizabeth Bowen. An evening's talk with the young people at Girton College gave her a sense of tingling and vitality; "one's angularities and obscurities are smoothed and lit" (1928).

January 15, 1941, she notes that Joyce is dead. "I remember Miss Weaver, in wool gloves, bringing *Ulysses* in typescript

to our teatable at Hogarth House. Roger I think sent her.
Would we devote our lives to printing it? The indecent pages
looked so incongruous: she was spinsterly, buttoned up. And
the pages reeled with indecency. I put it in the drawer of the
inlaid cabinet. One day Katherine Mansfield came, and I had
it out. She began to read, ridiculing: then suddenly said,
but there's something in this: a scene that should figure I
suppose in the history of literature. He was about the place,
but I never saw him. . . . I bought the blue paper book, and
read it here one summer I think with spasms of wonder, of
discovery, and then again with long lapses of intense boredom." It was in September, 1922, that she finished *Ulysses*,
and her *Diary* for September 6 contains a totally unsympa-
thetic appraisal. But a few weeks later (Sept. 26) she writes
down a talk with T. S. Eliot about *Ulysses*. "Tom said, 'He
is a purely literary writer. He is founded upon Walter Pater
with a dash of Newman.' I said he was virile—a he-goat; but
didn't expect Tom to agree. Tom did though; and said he left
out many things that were important. The book would be a
landmark, because it destroyed the whole of the 19th Century. It left Joyce himself with nothing to write another book
on. It showed up the futility of all the English styles. He
thought some of the writing beautiful. But there was no
'great conception'; that was not Joyce's intention. . . . But he
did not think that he gave a new insight into human nature—
said nothing new like Tolstoy. Bloom told one nothing. Indeed, he said, this new method of giving the psychology
proves to my mind that it doesn't work. It doesn't tell as
much as some casual glance from outside often tells. I said
I had found *Pendennis* more illuminating in this way. (The
horses are now cropping near my window; the little owl calling, and so I write nonsense.)"

And so we can see her opinions forming, while the owl calls
and the horses crop.

II

"I think," wrote Mrs. Woolf in the *Diary* on December 7, 1925, "I will find some theory about fiction; I shall read six novels and start some hares. The one I have in view is about *perspective.*" Two years later, writing about the novels of E. M. Forster, she declared that "if there is one gift more essential to a novelist than another it is the power of combination—the single vision. The success of the masterpieces seems to lie not so much in their freedom from faults—indeed we tolerate the grossest errors in them all—but in the immense persuasiveness of a mind which has completely mastered its perspective." [7] The idea is fully developed in the essay on *Robinson Crusoe* in *The Common Reader* II—a revision of an earlier review in the *Nation and Athenaeum,* February 6, 1926. There are two much-used ways of approaching a major classic like *Robinson Crusoe:* through the historical development of the novel and through the life of the author. But now and then as we use these methods of getting at a book, "a doubt insinuates itself—if we knew the very moment of Defoe's birth and whom he loved and why, if we had by heart the history of the origin, rise, growth, decline and fall of the English novel from its conception ... should we suck an ounce of additional pleasure from *Robinson Crusoe* or read it one whit more intelligently? For the book itself remains. However we may wind and wriggle, loiter and dally in our approach to books, a lonely battle waits us at the end. There is a piece of business to be transacted between writer and reader before any further dealings are possible, and to be reminded in the middle of this private interview that Defoe sold stockings, had brown hair, and was stood in the pillory, is a distraction and a worry. Our first task, and it is often formidable enough, is to master his perspective." We

7 *Atlantic Monthly,* November, 1927. Reprinted in *The Death of the Moth.*

must know how the novelist orders his world; climb upon
his shoulders, gaze through his eyes, until we understand "in
what order he ranges the large common objects upon which
novelists are fated to gaze: man and men; behind them
Nature; and above them that power which for convenience
and brevity we may call God." These apparently simple objects can be seen by people—even people living at the same
time and in the same place—with enormous differences in
proportion: human beings vast and trees minute to some;
Scott's mountains loom huge, Jane Austen picks out the roses
on the tea-cup; Peacock "bends over heaven and earth one
fantastic distorting mirror in which a tea-cup may be Vesuvius or Vesuvius a tea-cup," yet all three novelists lived
through the same years, in the same period of literary history.

Mastering the author's perspective as a preliminary to a
real appreciation of his novel sounds like a simple and in-
telligent process, but it isn't simple, because each reader has
his own perspective, developed from his own experiences and
prejudices; his own private harmony, achieved perhaps with
great effort, and cherished. And some authors so vigorously
inflict their own perspectives on us that we are insulted and
suffer boredom or agony. Yet if we recognize the source of
our anger or boredom, if, in short, we master our own perspective, a lasting delight may be born. Even if we do our
best, we as critics may end, when we sum up a writer, by
revealing some of the prejudices, the instincts, and the fallacies "out of which what it pleases us to call criticism is made"
—as Mrs. Woolf candidly remarks after a rather unsympa-
thetic review of Hemingway's stories. On the mind of every
reader of fiction some design has been traced. "Desires, appetites, however we may come by them, fill it in, scoring now
in this direction, now in that." [8] The world we create in
this way is always in process of creation and may be a very
personal one, "created in obedience to tastes that may be

8 "Phases of Fiction," in *Granite and Rainbow*.

peculiar to one temperament and distasteful to another."
Critics are readers, or at least are supposed to be; and Mrs.
Woolf certainly was; and she had a temperament and a
highly cultivated mind. She is not always successful as a
critic, either through failure to master her author's perspective or through distaste for that perspective. She tried hard
with Lawrence and Joyce, for instance. The *Diary*, October 2, 1932, finds her reading Lawrence's *Letters* "with the
usual sense of frustration," and she reflects that perhaps she
had too much in common with Lawrence: "the same pressure to be ourselves; so that I don't escape when I read him;
am suspended; what I want is to be made free of another
world. This Proust does. To me Lawrence is airless, con-
fined." She wanted no philosophy, no preaching, no repetition of the same idea. And she concludes very honestly, "I
haven't read him of course."

An article in the *Yale Review*, October, 1926, originally a
paper read at a school, and revised for *The Common Reader*
II under the title "How Should One Read a Book?" expresses
very simply some of the ideas about perspectives which she
later elaborated in a series of essays in the *Bookman*. "Here,
in *Robinson Crusoe*, we are trudging a plain high road; one
thing happens after another; the fact and the order of the fact
is enough. But if the open air and adventure mean everything to Defoe they mean nothing to Jane Austen. Here is
the drawing-room, and people talking, and by the many mirrors of their talk revealing their characters. And if, when we
have accustomed ourselves to the drawing-room and its reflections, we turn to Hardy, we are once more spun round.
The moors are round us and the stars are above our heads.
The other side of the mind is now exposed—the dark side
that comes uppermost in solitude, not the light side that
shows in company. Our relations are not towards people, but
towards Nature and destiny. Yet different as these worlds
are, each is consistent with itself. The maker of each is careful

D

to observe the laws of his own perspective, and however great
a strain they may put upon us they will never confuse us, as
lesser writers so frequently do, by introducing two different
kinds of reality into the same book. Thus to go from one
great novelist to another—from Jane Austen to Hardy, from
Peacock to Trollope, from Scott to Meredith—is to be
wrenched and uprooted; to be thrown this way and then
that." In "Phases of Fiction" [9] (the *Bookman*, April, May
and June, 1929), these brief suggestions are developed into
succinct critical appraisals of a score of major novelists, illuminated by some of her happiest images. She imagines a
mind at work on a shelf full of novels, choosing and rejecting
in accordance with its own appetites, and she begins with the
simplest appetite of all—the desire to believe in something
fictitious. She divides her novelists—they are mostly English,
with several French and Russian—into the Truthtellers, the
Romantics, the Character-Mongers and Comedians, the
Psychologists, the Satirists and Fantastics, and the Poets.
Speaking of Henry James's characters in *What Maisie Knew*,
she describes them as living "in a cocoon, spun from the
finest shades of meaning, which a society, completely un-
occupied by the business of getting its living, has time to spin
around and about itself." And of Proust: "The common stuff
of the book is made of this deep reservoir of perception. It is
from these depths that his characters rise, like waves forming,
then break and sink again into the moving sea of thought and
comment and analysis which gave them birth."

To return to the *Robinson Crusoe* essay, what might we
have expected on opening the story of a man on a desert
island? Certainly not what we got. "There are no sunsets and
no sunrises; there is no solitude and no soul. There is, on the
contrary, staring us full in the face, nothing but a large
earthenware pot"—a symbol for Defoe's genius for facts.
By means of this genius he "achieves effects that are beyond

9 Reprinted in *Granite and Rainbow*.

any but the great masters of descriptive prose." "A sense of desolation and of the deaths of many men is conveyed by remarking in the most prosaic way in the world, 'I never saw them afterwards, or any sign of them except three of their hats, one cap, and two shoes that were not fellows.' . . . Thus Defoe, by reiterating that nothing but a plain earthenware pot stands in the foreground, persuades us to see remote islands and the solitudes of the human soul. By believing fixedly in the solidity of the pot and its earthiness, he has subdued every other element to his design; he has roped the whole universe into harmony. And is there any reason, we ask as we shut the book, why the perspective that a plain earthenware pot exacts should not satisfy us as completely, once we grasp it, as man himself in all his sublimity standing against a background of broken mountains and tumbling oceans with stars flaming in the sky?"

In another essay on Defoe [10] there is an image relating Defoe to London. He belongs to the school of the great plain writers, "whose work is founded upon a knowledge of what is most persistent, though not most seductive, in human nature. The view of London from Hungerford Bridge, grey, serious, massive, and full of the subdued stir of traffic and business, prosaic if it were not for the masts of the ships and the towers and domes of the city, brings him to mind. The tattered girls with violets in their hands at the street corners, and the old weatherbeaten women patiently displaying their matches and bootlaces beneath the shelter of arches, seem like characters from his books." Virginia Woolf's love of London gave her one key to the art of Defoe.

Sir Walter Scott is one of the writers who, in her opinion, have entirely ceased to influence others, "who are enjoyed or neglected rather than criticised and read." The most impressionable beginner, "whose pen oscillates if exposed within a mile to the influence of Stendhal, Flaubert, Henry James,

10 *TLS*, April 24, 1919. Reprinted in *The Common Reader* I.

or Chekhov, can read the *Waverley Novels* without altering an adjective." She rereads *The Antiquary*. He used the wrong pen to describe the intricacies and passions of the heart, and as for his lovers, "as well talk of the hearts of seagulls and the passions and intricacies of walking-sticks and umbrellas ... A strong smell of camphor exudes from their poor dried breasts when, with a dismal croaking and cawing, they emit the astonishing language of their love-making." Yet his characters—though not his lovers—are alive only when they speak: "they never think; as for prying into their minds himself, or drawing inferences from their behaviour, Scott never attempted it.... If they stop talking it is to act. By their talk and by their acts—that is how we know them." So what is his perspective? "The emotions then in which Scott excels are not those of human beings pitted against other human beings, but of man in relation to fate. His romance is the romance of hunted men hiding in woods at night; of brigs standing out to sea; of waves breaking in the moonlight; of solitary sands and distant horsemen; of violence and suspense. And he is perhaps the last novelist to practise the great, the Shakespearean, art of making people reveal themselves in speech." [11]

The publication of a new edition of a writer's works calls for a comprehensive survey. "Jane Austen at Sixty," a review in the *Nation and Athenaeum*, December 15, 1923, of *The Works of Jane Austen*—incorporated in *The Common Reader*, I—is a sixteen-page essay. It is almost as if Mrs. Woolf had only the "book itself" to consider, undistracted by details of the author's biography. For Cassandra, Jane's sister, burned all letters except those she considered too trivial to be of interest. From the few letters that survive and a little gossip, Mrs. Woolf disengages Jane's personality, and then takes a look at *Love and Friendship*, written when Jane

11 "The Antiquary," *Nation and Athenaeum*, Nov. 22, 1924. Reprinted, revised, in *The Moment*.

was fifteen and intended for the schoolroom. Yet she was
already writing "for nobody, for our age, for her own," for
everybody—in short, she was *writing*; "one hears it in the
rhythm and shapeliness and severity of the sentences." And
as to the point of view, "the girl of fifteen is laughing, in her
corner, at the world." The unfinished and abandoned novel,
The Watsons, throws more light on her genius than the
polished masterpieces. One of Mrs. Woolf's ideas as a critic
is that the second-rate works of a major writer are the best
criticism of his major work. The first chapters are stiff
and bare; much preliminary drudgery must have preceded
the apparently effortless opening pages of her masterpieces.
"Those first angular chapters of *The Watsons* prove that
hers was not a prolific genius; she had not, like Emily
Brontë, merely to open the door to make herself felt." "Hum-
bly and gaily she collected the twigs and straws out of which
the nest was to be made and placed them neatly together.
The twigs and straws were a little dry and a little dusty in
themselves. There was the big house and the little house;
a tea party, a dinner party, and an occasional picnic; life was
hedged in by valuable connections and adequate incomes;
by muddy roads, wet feet, and a tendency on the part of the
ladies to get tired; a little money supported it, a little conse-
quence, and the education commonly enjoyed by upper
middle-class families living in the country. Vice, adventure,
passion were left outside. . . . One after another she creates
her fools, her prigs, her worldlings, her Mr. Collins', her Sir
Walter Elliotts, her Mrs. Bennetts. She encircles them with
the lash of a whip-like phrase which, as it runs round them,
cuts out their silhouettes for ever." Her wit has for partner
"the perfection of her taste. Her fool is a fool, her snob is
a snob, because he departs from the model of sanity and
sense which she has in mind, and conveys to us unmistakably
even while she makes us laugh. Never did any novelist make
more use of an impeccable sense of human values. It is

against the disc of an unerring heart, an unfailing good taste,
an almost stern morality, that she shows up those deviations
from kindness, truth, and sincerity which are among the most
delightful things in English literature." Her understanding
of her own powers and limitations made her immune to any
temptation from a Prince Regent to write historical novels;
and "she had all sorts of devices for evading scenes of passion. . . . The balance of her gifts was singularly perfect."

But she died at forty-two. Suppose she had lived on into
the later years which are often the most interesting in a
writer's career. Mrs. Woolf examines the last completed
novel, *Persuasion*, in the light of the books she might have
written. What of Jane Austen at sixty? *Persuasion* has a peculiar beauty, and also the peculiar dullness that often marks
the transition between two periods in an author's work. A
new element in *Persausion* comes through Anne Elliott's
beginning to discover that the world is larger and more mysterious than she had supposed. She notices things that suggest an alteration in Jane Austen's own attitude to life; for
she is seeing life largely through the eyes of a woman who
"unhappy herself, has a special sympathy for the happiness
and unhappiness of others, which, until the very end, she is
forced to comment upon in silence." There is the famous
conversation about woman's constancy, which proves "not
merely the biographical fact that Jane Austen had loved, but
the aesthetic fact that she was no longer afraid to say so."
The experience had sunk in deeply enough to be used in
fiction, and she was ready to use it by 1817. Had she lived
there would have been changes in her life; she was becoming
famous; she would have lived much more outside the quiet
country cottage; she was beginning "to feel confidence in
her own success." Probably her comedy would have suffered,
her sense of security been shaken, her knowledge of the complexity of human nature been increased. "She would have
devised a method, clear and composed as ever, but deeper

and more suggestive, for conveying not only what people say, but what they leave unsaid; not only what they are, but what life is." She would have been the forerunner of Proust, of Henry James. As it was, she remains "the most perfect artist among women."

The perspective of a novelist does not necessarily remain fixed. Conrad's, for instance.[12] In the foreground of the earlier tales are the "everlasting children of the sea," known and loved by Conrad the sea captain, interpreted by the other Conrad who was that "discreet and understanding man," Marlow, introspective and analytical. And these characters play out their destinies against a background of ships "first and foremost, ships at anchor, ships flying before the storm, ships in harbour;" and sunsets and dawns and the "gaudy brilliancy of Eastern ports." When Conrad retired from the sea, and felt after finishing the last story in the *Typhoon* volume that there was nothing more to write about, Marlow (Mrs. Woolf fancies) may have reminded him that, though he may have said the last word about Captain Whalley and his relation to the universe, "there remained on shore a number of men and women whose relationships, though of a more personal kind, might be worth looking into. If we further suppose that there was a volume of Henry James on board and that Marlow gave his friend the book to take to bed with him, we may seek support in the fact that it was in 1905 that Conrad wrote a very fine essay upon that master." Marlow for some years became the dominant partner—the years of *Nostromo, Chance, The Arrow of Gold.* He was advising his other self to shift his angle of vision; "the human heart is more intricate than the forest." The Russians have a proverb that the heart is a dark forest. The phrase "the heart of darkness," title of one of Conrad's great stories,

12 "Joseph Conrad," *TLS*, Aug. 14, 1924. Reprinted in *The Common Reader* I.

exercised a special fascination over Virginia Woolf's imagination, occurring in her novels a number of times. "If as novelist you wish to test man in all his relationships, the proper antagonist is man; his ordeal is in society, not solitude." Conrad, Mrs. Woolf thinks, was never able after the middle period to "bring his figures into perfect relation with their background. He never believed in his later and more highly sophisticated characters as he had believed in his early seamen." His creed was that the world rests upon a very few simple ideas, among them the idea of fidelity. In the more crowded and complicated world of his later novels he was never sure of the values tested in the ordeals of the sea. Could "complex men and women of many interests and relations" be tried by them? "There are no masts in drawing-rooms; the typhoon does not test the worth of politicians and business men. Seeking and not finding such supports, the world of Conrad's later period has about it an involuntary obscurity, an inconclusiveness, almost a disillusionment which baffles and fatigues." This interpretation of a shift in Conrad's perspective may not be satisfactory, but it does invite testing by rereading. Perhaps Conrad did not believe as fully in the world of *Chance* as he did in that of *The Nigger of the Narcissus*. The storyteller's belief in the men and women he creates is a conviction which the earlier Conrad shares with Chaucer—as Mrs. Woolf incidentally points out in an essay devoted mainly to the fifteenth-century Paston family.[13] (Sir John Paston had Chaucer in his library, and he read him too.) Chaucer's people are animated by his conviction. His young girls, for instance, have a stability about them, showing that he has made up his mind about them and the world they live in; there is no blurring, no hesitation; he can get on with his story; "paint knights and squires, good women and bad, cooks, shipmen, priests, and we will supply the landscape, give his society its belief, its

13 "The Pastons and Chaucer," *The Common Reader* I.

standing towards life and death, and make of the journey to Canterbury a spiritual pilgrimage."

Conrad and Chaucer: It is characteristic of Mrs. Woolf's own perspective as reader-critic to bring together two writers far apart in time, because of some resemblance or contrast; thus creating the impression that the vast landscape of letters is always there, to be seen when she lifts her eyes from the little corner she is examining—as she looked out the window in the ideal library where she was reading, down a long corridor of English literature and life. In the essay "On Not Knowing Greek" [14] we meet Jane Austen and Sophocles —Emma Woodhouse and Electra. Electra is a figure "so tightly bound that she can only move an inch this way and an inch that. But each movement must tell to the utmost." Her words in a crisis—mere cries of despair, joy, hate—"give angle and outline to the play." So, with a thousand differences of degree, Jane Austen's Emma, saying "I will dance with you" marks a moment in the shape of the novel which "rises higher than the rest, which, though not eloquent in itself, or violent, or made striking by beauty of language, has the whole weight of the book behind it." Jane Austen's figures, like those of Sophocles, are bound and she, too, "in her modest, everyday prose, chose the dangerous art where one slip means death." Or discussing in the same essay Aeschylus and the ambiguity of the highest poetry: the meaning is on the far side of language; "it is the meaning that Dostoevsky (hampered as he was by prose and as we are by translation) leads us to by some astonishing run up the scale of emotions, and points at but cannot indicate; the meaning that Shakespeare succeeds in snaring." Or take "Notes on an Elizabethan Play" [15] (Ford's *'Tis Pity She's a Whore*), and that hard-pressed heroine Annabella. What do we really know about that spirited girl? Of character she has not a

---

14 *The Common Reader* I.
15 *The Common Reader* I.

trace, and nobody describes her, and "she is always at the height of her passion, never at its approach." Then, surprisingly, we are invited to compare her with Anna Karenina, who also has crises of passion and despair, and the comparison points up the difference between poetry and prose, the play and the novel. "The dramatist goes behind the single and the separate, shows us not Annabella in love, but love itself; not Anna Karenina throwing herself under the train, but ruin and death and the '... soul, like a ship in a black storm / driven I know not whither.' "

Bring together Henry James—"that courtly, worldly, sentimental old gentleman," who can "still make us afraid of the dark"—and Mrs. Radcliffe, who made our ancestors shudder. If you wish to guess what they felt when they read *The Mysteries of Udolpho* "you cannot do better than read *The Turn of the Screw*." The new fear resembles the old. "But what is it that we are afraid of? We are not afraid of ruins, or moonlight, or ghosts. Indeed, we should be relieved to find that Quint and Miss Jessel are ghosts.... The odious creatures are much closer to us than ghosts have ever been. The governess is not so much frightened of them as of the sudden extension of her own field of perception, which in this case widens to reveal to her the presence all about her of an unmentionable evil. The appearance of the figures is an illustration, not in itself specially alarming, of a state of mind which is profoundly mysterious and terrifying.... The oncoming of the state is preceded not by the storms and howlings of the old romances, but by an absolute hush and lapse of nature which we feel to represent the ominous trances of her own mind.... The horror of the story comes from the force with which it makes us realize the power that our minds possess for such excursions into the darkness; when certain lights sink or certain barriers are lowered, the ghosts of the

mind, untracked desires, indistinct intimations, are seen to
be a large company." [16]

After we have discovered the author's perspective from
reading his work, our curiosity is aroused about how he came
to see things in that particular relationship, and we are led
to biographical speculation. Mrs. Woolf satisfies our curiosity
in numberless ways, often incidentally. Take, for instance,
the influence of Mary Wollstonecraft's circumstances upon
her opinions. She was Jane Austen's contemporary: "If Jane
Austen had lain as a child on the landing to prevent her
father from thrashing her mother, her soul might have burnt
with such a passion against tyranny that all her novels might
have been consumed in one cry for justice." That had been
Mary Wollstonecraft's first experience of the "joys of married life." No wonder she refused to marry Imlay, though she
loved him passionately and pursued him till he could not endure it and was always disappearing. "Tickling minnows he
had hooked a dolphin, and the creature rushed him through
the waters till he was dizzy and only wanted to escape." Experiences of sordid misery led her to believe that nothing
mattered to a woman but independence. When the French
Revolution came, expressing her deepest theories and convictions, she was ready to dash off "those two eloquent and
daring books—the *Reply to Burke* and the *Vindication of the
Rights of Women*, which are so true that they seem now to
contain nothing new in them—their originality had become
our commonplace." [17]

"Somewhere, everywhere, now hidden, now apparent in
whatever is written down is the form of a human being. If
we seek to know him, are we idly occupied?" Sir Thomas
Browne was the first English writer to "rouse this particular

16 *Granite and Rainbow,* "Henry James's Ghost Stories" and "The
Supernatural in Fiction," reprinted from *TLS,* Dec. 22, 1921, and
Jan. 31, 1918.
17 "Mary Wollstonecraft," *The Common Reader* II.

confusion with any briskness." The confusion, one supposes, of the genetic fallacy, how something came to be with what it is. The question does not present itself so acutely with a poet and scarcely at all with the Greeks and Latins. "The poet gives us his essence, but prose takes the mould of the body and mind entire." [18] Mrs. Woolf looks at the question again in "Personalities," [19] which takes off from a remark by Symonds that he disliked Keats's personality. Critics tell us that we should be impersonal when we criticize, and it is easy to be that with Greeks like Aeschylus and Sappho, because we know practically nothing about them except how they died—which happened to be in a startling fashion. We have only their work, cut off from us by time and language, pure from contamination. Suppose Tennyson had been killed on the steps of St. Paul's by a stone dropped by an eagle; or George Eliot had gathered her skirts about her and leaped from a cliff like Sappho. Think what a library of comment and psychological speculation and facts about how it happened and who saw it all would have been written. Some great artists, whether much or little is known about them, remain inscrutable—Jane Austen in her small way, Shakespeare in his great—for they have infused the whole of themselves in their work. The imperfect artists do not do that, and their personality becomes something to like or dislike. And then, characteristically, she qualifies the statement, for there is Keats, a great artist, whose personality nevertheless affects us. Our likes and dislikes for authors are as varied and as little accountable as for people in the flesh. She mentioned some of her own in a letter to the *Nation*, September 12, 1925 (reprinted in *The Moment*): "Questions of affection are of course always disputable. I can only reiterate that while I would cheerfully become Shakespeare's cat, Scott's pig, or Keats's canary, if by so doing I could share the society

18 "Reading," *The Captain's Death Bed.*
19 *The Moment, and Other Essays.*

of these great men, I would not cross the road (reasons of curiosity apart) to dine with Wordsworth, Byron, or Dickens. Yet I venerate their genius." And she adds that this only means that "writers have characters apart from their books, which are sympathetic to some, antithetic to others." A pretense to scientific detachment is quite foreign to Mrs. Woolf's temperament. She fancies that it would be rather alarming to be left alone with Jane Austen, but quite pleasant to find Charlotte Brontë at home—"her very faults make a breach through which one steps to intimacy." As for writers, "some show themselves, others hide themselves, irrespective of their greatness." To conclude, Mrs. Woolf would probably agree that working with the biographical approach to criticism may be irrelevant to an appraisal of an author's works; or it may throw valuable light on his perspective—on his values, his beliefs, his handicaps—and so enhance our understanding and our pleasure. It may also be so interesting in itself as a human story that the work itself is simply an incident in the story. It may offer the excitement of following clues, solving mysteries, detecting forgeries. Only if we think that we have evaluated the work of art by tracing its genesis do we, as critics, miss the boat and commit the genetic fallacy.

III

If an earthenware pot sits in the foreground of Defoe's landscape, the Soul has the central place in the Russian picture, which English readers and critics thought they were looking at, from about 1912, when Constance Garnett's translation of *The Brothers Karamazov* appeared, until the disconcerting progress of the Bolshevik Revolution began to alter the perspective. There had been occasional references to the "mysterious soul of Russia" after the publication of Melchior de Vogüé's book on the Russian novel in the late

1880's, but it did not become a kind of cult until the Garnett translations revealed the genius of Dostoevsky. The Ballet Russe and the Russian opera, Diaghilev and Nijinsky, Stravinsky and Chaliapin, had captured the imagination of the English art and music lovers before the 1914 War. And since in the early days of the war Russia was an ally not too easily accepted by the more skeptical—among whom was Bernard Shaw—it was very satisfactory to have political realities blurred by the mystical conception of the Soul. Translations of Russian authors multiplied. Books were published with such titles as *The Slav Soul, The Soul of Russia, The Russian Soul,* and writers like Havelock Ellis, Rebecca West, and Middleton Murry were feverish with enthusiasm for the spiritual qualities of the Russian people and their literature.

Any complete account of Virginia Woolf's opinions about Russian fiction would have to include all the scattered references in her *Diary* and her book reviews, as well as the familiar essays in *The Common Reader* I—"Modern Fiction" and "The Russian Point of View"—and the Tolstoy and Dostoevsky passages in "Phases of Fiction." Hers was no passing enthusiasm. As late as March, 1940, she noted in the *Diary:* "I read Tolstoy at breakfast—Goldenweiser [Goldenveizer?] that I translated with Kot in 1923 and have almost forgotten.[20] Always the same reality—like touching an exposed electric wire. Even so imperfectly conveyed—his rugged short cut mind—to me the most, not sympathetic, but inspiring, rousing: genius in the raw. Thus more disturbing, more 'shocking,' more of a thunderclap, even on art, even on literature, than any other writer." That had been her feeling, she recalls, years before, about *War and Peace,* just now (1940) undergoing a great revival in England. A *TLS* article, referring to its popularity, had quoted her on the Russian Soul (March 23, 1940). "Kot" was S. S. Koteliansky, who translated several books published by the Hogarth Press in

20 *Talks with Tolstoy,* by A. B. Goldenveizer (Hogarth Press, 1923).

1922 and 1923. Mr. Leonard Woolf wrote of him at the time of his death in 1955 that "at one time or another Lawrence, Katherine Mansfield, Virginia Woolf, and I collaborated with him in translating books by Tolstoy, Dostoevsky, Chekhov, Gorky and Bunin.... His method was to write out the translation in his own strange English and leave a large space between the lines in which I then turned his English into my English.... You only learned to the full Kot's intensity and integrity by collaborating with him in a Russian translation." [21] Mrs. Woolf did not know Russian, but she and her husband "taught ourselves a little Russian in order to be able to understand Koteliansky's problems in translating.... Mrs. Woolf went through the text with him, sentence by sentence, and then put the translation into good English." [22]

Mrs. Woolf wrote reviews of Russian translations from 1917 to 1922, chiefly in the *TLS*, and of course anonymously. Some parts of them were revised and used in the essays in *The Common Reader*; but about a dozen have not so far been reprinted in any of the posthumous volumes. They are fresh and perceptive, and stand up well in comparison with her better known criticism of Tolstoy, Dostoevsky, Chekhov, and Turgenev; and since it is not always convenient to search back files of the *TLS*, they will be briefly discussed later. In the *TLS* for April 10, 1919, she wrote on "Modern Novels"— slightly revised in *The Common Reader* (1925) with the title "Modern Fiction." She labeled her contemporaries— Wells, Bennett, Galsworthy—"materialists," because in her opinion they wrote of unimportant things and spent immense skill and industry "making the trivial and the transitory appear the true and the enduring." "Life," she says, "escapes; and perhaps without life nothing else is worth while.... Whether we call it life or spirit, truth or reality, this, the essential thing, has moved off, or on, and refuses to be con-

21 *New Statesman and Nation*, Feb. 5, 1955.
22 *A Bibliography of Virginia Woolf*, p. 77.

tained any longer in such ill-fitting vestments as we provide."
She was of course expressing her own need to find new
techniques for what she wished to say about life. And what
is life? "Not a series of gig lamps symmetrically arranged;
but a luminous halo, a semi-transparent envelope surrounding us from the beginning of consciousness to the end." The
task of the novelist is to convey "this unknown and un-
circumscribed spirit" with as little mixture as possible of the
alien and external. Discussing one of Chekhov's stories, she
says that she cannot avoid, even in making the most ele-
mentary remarks on English fiction, mentioning the Russian
influence. To write of any fiction save theirs is a waste of
time; "if we want understanding of the soul and heart where
shall we find it of comparable profundity?" Her own tem-
perature begins to rise, and she discerns the features of a
saint in every great Russian writer. "It is the saint in them
which confounds us with a feeling of our own irreligious
triviality, and turns so many of our novels to tinsel and
trickery." The questions they ask, to which there seems no
answer, induce a sort of resentful despair. But perhaps we do
see something that escapes them. Our voice of protest is
"the voice of another and an ancient civilization which seems
to have bred in us the instinct to enjoy and fight rather than
to suffer and understand." Deductions from a comparison of
two fictions "so immeasurably far apart" are futile, except
as the comparison opens up the infinite possibilities of the
art—in method, experiment, feeling, thought, perception. In
the paper Mrs. Woolf read to the Heretics, Cambridge,
May 18, 1924, the "spirit we live by" acquires a symbol in
Mrs. Brown, the little elderly lady, enigmatic, who sits in a
corner of the railway carriage on the way from Richmond to
Waterloo. How capture the essential Mrs. Brown? The English writer would try to do it one way, the French another.
"The Russian would pierce through the flesh; would reveal
the soul—the soul alone, wandering out into the Waterloo

Road, asking of life some tremendous question which would sound on and on in our ears after the book was finished." [23]

"The Russian Point of View" attempts to define the Soul as it appears in the fiction of Dostoevsky and Chekhov, on which the English have "feasted" for twenty years, depending on translators and thus trying to judge a literature "stripped of its style." Mrs. Woolf is less than fair in saying that our estimate of the qualities of Russian fiction had been formed by critics "who have never read a word of Russian, or seen Russia, or even heard the language spoken by natives." From the 1860's on, and increasingly after 1900, there had been translations and interpretations by critics who knew the language and the people and the country; among them Constance and Edward Garnett, the American Isabel Hapgood, Charles Turner, Maurice Baring, and Aylmer Maude.[24] But broadly speaking, of course, translations are imperfect substitutes for the original. Difference in values as well as in language separates the English from the Russians. The first impression of Chekhov on the English reader is one of bewilderment. Why does he make a story out of this little episode? What about the inconclusiveness of the ending? It is all so different from our assumptions about stories; the tune is unfamiliar, the harmony incomplete, the emphasis falls in odd places. Mrs. Woolf wonders if he is primarily interested "not in the soul's relation with other souls, but with the soul's relation to health—with the soul's relation to goodness. . . . The soul is ill; the soul is cured; the soul is not cured. Those are the emphatic points in his stories." The method that seemed at first casual and inconclusive finally appears "the result of an exquisitely original and fastidious taste . . . controlled by an honesty for which we can find no match save among the Russians themselves." The soul is the

23 "Mr. Bennett and Mrs. Brown," reprinted in *The Captain's Death Bed.*

24 See *East-West Passage,* by Dorothy Brewster, pp. 142 ff.

E

chief character in Russian fiction; "delicate and subtle in
Chekhov, subject to an infinite number of humours and
distempers, it is of greater depth and volume in Dostoevsky,
liable to violent diseases and raging fevers, but still the pre-
dominant concern." This soul has little sense of humor, no
sense of comedy; and Mrs. Woolf, with her gift of imagery,
becomes hopelessly involved in seething whirlpools, water-
spouts, and gyrating sandstorms, into which she is sucked,
"blinded, suffocated, and at the same time filled with a
giddy rapture." Then a rope is thrown to us, we hold on,
now submerged, but "now in a moment of vision understanding more than we have ever understood before." Nothing is outside Dostoevsky's province, and "out it tumbles
upon us, hot, scalding, mixed, marvellous, terrible, oppressive
—the human soul."

"But one can't read D. again," she noted in the *Diary*,
August 16, 1933, "having been reading Turgenev," who
wrote and rewrote, "to clear the truth of the unessential.
But Dostoevsky would say that everything matters." She was
in complete sympathy with Turgenev. Her insight into the
method and form of his novels in the essay "The Novels of
Turgenev" [25] is evidence not only of her sympathy but also
of his influence upon her own writing.[26] Reviewing in the
TLS (Dec. 8, 1921) the Garnett translation of *The Two
Friends and Other Stories*, she asks how he secures his effects,
and what sort of world did he create. "Beyond the circle of
his scene seems to lie a great space which flows in at the window, presses upon people, isolates them, makes them incapable of action, indifferent to effect; sincere and open-
minded. Some background of that sort is common to much
of Russian literature. But Turgenev adds to this scene a

25 *TLS*, Dec. 14, 1933. Reprinted in *Yale Review*, December, 1933,
and in *The Captain's Death Bed*.
26 See Gilbert Phelps, *The Russian Novel in English Fiction*, pp.
132–37, and Brewster, *East-West Passage*, pp. 223–24.

quality we find nowhere else"—and she quotes a drawing-room scene where at the end a woman goes to the window and remarks that the moon must have risen; there is moonlight on the tops of the poplars. With his remarkable emotional power Turgenev "draws together the moon and the group around the samovar, the voices and the flowers and the warmth of the garden—he fuses them in one moment of great intensity, though all round are the silent spaces, and he turns away, in the end, with a little shrug of his shoulders." Mrs. Woolf's characters have a way of going to the window, turning away from the intimate and personal concerns, and shifting their gaze to "life in general."

Turgenev's novels have form, in the sense that "one thing follows another rightly" (*Diary*, Aug. 16, 1933). But what things? Events? "Turgenev did not see his books as a succession of events; he saw them as a succession of emotions radiating from some character at the centre.... The connexion is not of events but of emotions, and if at the end of the book we feel a sense of completeness, it must be that in spite of his defects as a storyteller, Turgenev's ear for emotion was so fine that even if he uses an abrupt contrast, or passes away from his people to a description of the sky or of the forest, all is held together by the truth of his insight. He never distracts us with the real incongruity—the introduction of an emotion that is false, or a transition that is arbitrary." [27] Some years before (1922) Mrs. Woolf, in commenting on Lubbock's *The Craft of Fiction*, had expressed dissatisfaction with the term "form" as applied to a novel; it belonged to the visual arts; "significant form" meant something precise to her artist friends. But the "book itself" does not have form which you see, but emotion which you feel. The emotion must be tranquillized, ordered, and composed, and this is accomplished by what she prefers to call "art." [28]

27 "The Novels of Turgenev."
28 "On Re-reading Novels," reprinted in *The Moment*.

In several early reviews of stories by Dostoevsky, Mrs.
Woolf, not being bowled over by his genius in these minor
works, has some pertinent criticisms to make.[29] When he is
fully possessed by his intuition, "he is able to read the most
inscrutable writings at the depths of the darkest souls; but
when it deserts him, the whole of his amazing machinery
seems to spin fruitlessly in the air." "Dostoevsky at Cranford" is the intriguing title of a review of *The Honest Thief
and Other Stories*. They are provincial tales, and so the fancy
is not farfetched. How would Dostoevsky have behaved himself on the vicarage lawn? In "Uncle's Dream" the little
town bears a superficial likeness to Cranford: the ladies drink
tea and talk scandal, and Dostoevsky finds it all amusing
enough and then grows impatient, and it would be idle to
expect that he would linger in the High Street or "hang in a
rapture of observation round the draper's shop." Yet the little
town aroused in him, "as human life so seldom did, his sense
of comedy"—more like that of Wycherley than that of Jane
Austen; a comedy that rapidly runs to seed and becomes ex-
travagant farce. Perhaps it is because we know so little about
the family history of the Cranford ladies that we can put
the book down with a smile. "Still we need not underrate the
value of comedy because Dostoevsky makes the perfection of
the English product appear to be the result of leaving out all
the most important things."

Rash generalizations about the Russians were common
during this early period of fascinated discovery of Russian
literature, and Mrs. Woolf makes her contribution in two
reviews—one of Tolstoy's *The Cossacks* (Feb. 1, 1917) and
the other of Chekhov's *The Bishop and Other Stories* (Aug.
14, 1919). She envies the Russians "that extraordinary union
of extreme simplicity combined with the utmost subtlety

29 *TLS*, Feb. 22 and Oct. 11, 1917, and Oct. 23, 1919. The story
collections reviewed are *The Eternal Husband, The Gambler, The Honest Thief*.

which seems to mark both the educated Russian and the peasant equally"; and the peasants in Chekhov's stories: "each obscure and brutish mind has had rubbed in it a little transparency through which the spirit shines amazingly." (There is a saving "seems.") She can be amusing about the Russian sense of brotherhood—another popular generalization—"a sense hardly to be found in English literature." The English seem embarrassed when they try to say "brother"; the nearest equivalent is "mate"—and that doesn't sound spiritual.

New volumes of the Garnett translation of Chekhov kept appearing to satisfy a large and inquisitive public; and as he became better known he seemed more on a level with the English; for one thing, he was not heroic. He was always questioning, leaving us with a queer feeling that the solid ground upon which we expected to make a landing has been twitched from under us, leaving us asking questions in midair. But he is a born storyteller, with great originality in the choice of elements, hinting at a new arrangement; and he has already made us alive to the fact that inconclusive endings are legitimate; "though they leave us feeling melancholy and perhaps uncertain,. yet somehow or other they provide a resting point for the mind—a solid object casting the shade of reflection and speculation." Can we now treat Chekhov as we treat a writer in our own tongue? "We want to understand the great sum of things which a writer takes for granted, which is the background of his thought; for if we can imagine that, the figures in the foreground, the pattern he has wrought upon it, will be more easily intelligible." She then contrasts the English and Russian backgrounds, the English rather cozy, the Russian steppe vast. In Chekhov's story *The Steppe*, "as the travellers move slowly over the immense space, now stopping at an inn, now overtaking some shepherd or wagon, it seems to be the journey of the Russian soul, and the empty space, so sad and so passionate, becomes the background of his thought. The stories themselves in their inconclusiveness and their intimacy, appear to be the result of a chance meeting on a lonely road.... Take away the orderly civilization; look from your window upon nothing but the empty steppe, feel towards each human being that he is a traveller who will be seen once and never again, and then life of itself is so terrible and marvellous that no fantastic colouring is necessary." [30] (But one remembers that Egdon Heath and the Yorkshire moors are not exactly cozy.)

Mrs. Woolf concludes "The Russian Point of View" with Tolstoy—the greatest of all novelists, for "what else can we call the author of *War and Peace*?" At first sight he seems to see what we see, and he proceeds as we do, from the outside inward, and nothing seems to go unobserved or unrecorded. "And what his infallible eye reports of a cough or a trick of the hands his infallible brain refers to something hidden in the character, so that we know his people, not only by the way they love and their views on politics and the immortality of the soul, but also by the way they sneeze and choke." Life dominates Tolstoy. But "at the centre of all the brilliant and flashing petals of the flower, this scorpion, 'Why live?'" His Pierre or his Levin "turns the world round between his fingers, and never ceases to ask even as he enjoys it, what is the meaning of it, and what should be our aims." The world turns to dust and ashes and fear mingles with our pleasure. Of the three great Russians, "it is Tolstoy who most enthralls us and most repels." It seems that it would take the joy out of life to meet the Russian Soul, wandering in the Waterloo Road, asking the ultimate question.

IV

There is a note in the *Diary* (March 22, 1928) about a plan to write some "nice little discreet" articles for twenty-

[30] Quotations from *TLS* reviews, May 16, 1918, and Aug. 14, 1919.

five pounds each month—"and so live; without stress; and read what I want to." One of these little articles may have been the delightful "Dr. Burney's Evening Party," which first appeared in the New York *Herald Tribune Books* in 1929.[31] Most of the facts about the party come from Fanny Burney's *Diary;* but out of them Mrs. Woolf creates a scene of the liveliest comedy and a memorable picture of Dr. Johnson. Here we have Fanny herself, Dr. Burney, Daddy Crisp, Piozzi, Mrs. Thrale, the aristocratic Fulke Greville, other friends and members of the family—and above all Dr. Johnson, who was expected to talk. The party, planned with such good intentions, ended disastrously. Dr. Johnson communed with his own mind. Signor Piozzi played the piano; the Burney daughters sang duets, and Piozzi went to sleep. "Dr. Johnson explored still further the resources of his mind," sitting looking at the fire, with his back to the piano, while Fulke Greville stood "superciliously upon the hearth-rug. And the night was cold." Dr. Johnson may have seemed lost in thought, but was not unaware. He suddenly roused himself—"his 'starts of vision' were always astonishing and almost always painful. . . . He suddenly uttered the words for which the company had been waiting all the evening." He demolished Fulke Greville. The Burney children said afterward that it was as good as a comedy.

Essays that appeared first in *The Common Reader*—in 1925 or 1932—must often have been written as a result of reading what she wanted to, not what she was asked to review. On November 16, 1931, she was furbishing up two long Elizabethan articles to front a new *Common Reader*. She could have rummaged in what she called the Elizabethan Lumber Room and found many strange things that had fascinated her in her early reading of Hakluyt—"not so much a book as a great bundle of commodities loosely tied together, an emporium, a lumber room strewn with ancient sacks,

31 Reprinted in *The Common Reader* II.

obsolete nautical instruments, huge bales of wool, and little bags of rubies and emeralds. One is forever untying this packet here, sampling that heap over there, wiping the dust off some vast map of the world, and sitting down in semi-darkness to sniff the strange smells of silks and leathers and ambergris, while outside tumble the huge waves of the uncharted Elizabethan seas." The narratives of these traffics and discoveries inspired in part the greatest age of English poetry; but the effect on English prose was not beneficial. Compare a passage from Montaigne with one from Sidney's *Defence of Poesie*. Sidney and Montaigne were contemporaries, but an age seems to separate them. The Elizabethan prose writer "tripped and stumbled over the convolutions of his own rich draperies." Mrs. Woolf writes about Sidney's *Arcadia* in a way that almost makes one want to read it. But his grasp on his "ambling phantoms" loosens and becomes slack and so does the tie between writer and reader, and the book "floats away into the thin air of limbo. It becomes one of those half-forgotten and deserted places where the grasses grow over fallen statues and the rain drips and the marble steps are green with moss and vast weeds flourish in the flower-beds. And yet it is a beautiful garden to wander in now and then; one stumbles over lovely broken faces, and here and there a flower blooms and the nightingale sings in the lilac tree." But in the *Arcadia*, "as in some luminous globe, all the seeds of English fiction lie latent." In a concise final paragraph she traces the possibilities of the development of the English novel, in the form of questions stirred by the *Arcadia*; and she concludes: "But as if Sidney knew that he had broached a task too large for his youth to execute, had bequeathed a legacy for other ages to inherit, he put down his pen, mid-way, and left unfinished in all its beauty and absurdity this attempt to while away the long days at Wilton, telling a story to his sister." [32]

32 "The Countess of Pembroke's *Arcadia*," *The Common Reader* II.

Among the "strange Elizabethans" [33] is the obscure sister of Gabriel Harvey, the friend of Sir Philip Sidney and of Spenser, who lived to a great age for an Elizabethan; who kept a commonplace book; who suffered a conflict between the "Harvey who blundered among men and the Harvey who sat wisely at home among his books. The one who acts and suffers brings his case to the one who reads and thinks for advice and consolation." He returned in the end to his native village, an old and disappointed scholar, living in complete obscurity at Saffron Walden, but gave us a better chance to know him than most Elizabethans; "when we say that Harvey lived we mean that he quarreled and was tiresome and ridiculous and struggled and failed and had a face like ours—a changing, a variable, a human face." Mrs. Woolf approaches Harvey through his sister, a milkmaid, who was wooed—but not for marriage—by a young nobleman and who wrote about it to her brother, then a young Cambridge student. He kept her letters. We go astray badly in the field of ordinary daily Elizabethan life, because Elizabethan prose, for all its "beauty and bounty," was a very imperfect medium, "still scarcely separated off from the body of its poetry." Harvey possessed to some extent "the modern instinct for preserving trifles, for keeping copies of letters, and for making notes of ideas that struck him in the margins of books. If we rummage among these fragments we shall, at any rate, leave the highroad and perhaps hear some roar of laughter from a tavern door, where poets are drinking; or meet humble people going about their milking and their love-making without a thought that this is the great Elizabethan age, or that Shakespeare is at this moment strolling down the Strand and might tell one, if one plucked him by the sleeve, to whom he wrote the sonnets, and what he meant by Hamlet." The first person we meet off the highroad is Mercy Harvey, milking in the fields near Saffron Walden,

33 "The Strange Elizabethans," *The Common Reader* II.

on a day in 1574. The story unfolds, luckily discovered by her brother in time to save her honor. Mercy's romance is broken off; "the clouds descend again; and we no longer see the milkmaid, the old woman, the treacherous servingman who came with malmsey and cakes and rings and ribbons to tempt a poor girl's honor while she milked her cows." No uncommon story probably; it just happens that we have her own account to her brother. But what particularly interests Virginia Woolf is the language of the letters: "the sway of the Elizabethan convention was so strong, the accent of their speech was so masterful, that she bears herself with a grace and expresses herself with a resonance that would have done credit to a woman of birth and literary training"—as the few quotations prove. "Mercy the milkmaid writes a natural and noble style, which is incapable of vulgarity, and equally incapable of intimacy." It is this last quality that makes it so difficult for us to get the feeling of daily life. The daughter of the Duke of Northumberland, stating her claim for a better room to sleep in at court, writes as badly as Mercy the milkmaid writes well, and equally fails to give us the sense of intimacy, the background of Elizabethan life. It is because Harvey kept that commonplace book that we seem to see his face so clearly.

Reviewing Dorothy Osborne's *Letters*, Mrs. Woolf observed that in English literature there is a bare season— "sometimes like early spring in our country-side"—when the trees stand out and the hills are not muffled in green, and it is very different from June, with its tremors and murmurs and the smallest wood full of movement. So in English literature "we have to wait till the sixteenth century is over and the seventeenth well on its way before the bare landscape becomes full of stir and quiver and we can fill in the spaces between the great books with the voices of people talking." [34]

From the rather incidental suggestions in a number of her

34 *The Common Reader* II.

essays, it is clear that Mrs. Woolf could have written a history of English literature—"how one age follows another and one influence cancels another"—that orderly progression so efficiently taught in universities, as she had noted with some misgiving. It was people, not theories and generalizations, that fascinated the novelist-critic. As early as 1925 she was playing with the idea of writing a book to be called *Lives of the Obscure*—"to tell the whole history of England in one obscure life after another" (*Diary*, July 20 and Sept. 22).

v

Mrs. Woolf's preference among writers of memoirs and autobiographies, expressed as early as 1916, was for the less important people; "the men and women who set out with no excuse except perhaps that they saw the Duke of Wellington once, to confide to us their opinions, their quarrels, their aspirations, and their diseases, generally end by becoming, for the time at least, actors in those private dramas with which we beguile our solitary walks and our sleepless hours." [35] The preference persisted and she wrote in 1939: "Since so much is known that used to be unknown, the question now inevitably asks itself, whether the lives of great men only should be recorded. Is not anyone who has lived a life, and left a record of that life, worthy of biography—the failures as well as the successes, the humble as well as the illustrious?" [36]

In *A Room of One's Own*, discussing the possible material open to the woman novelist, she thinks of the "infinitely obscure lives" of the majority of women, which remain to be recorded. She walks through the streets of London, "feeling in imagination the pressure of dumbness, the accumulation of unrecorded life, whether from the women at the street

35 *TLS*, Nov. 30, 1916. Reprinted in *Granite and Rainbow*.
36 *Atlantic Monthly*, April, 1939, "The Art of Biography." Reprinted in *The Death of the Moth*.

corners with their arms akimbo, and the rings embedded in their fat swollen fingers, talking with a gesticulation like the swing of Shakespeare's words; or from the violet-sellers and match-sellers and old crones stationed under doorways; or from drifting girls whose faces, like waves in sun and cloud, signal the coming of men and women and the flickering lights of shop windows."

But some records of obscure lives must survive, if the critic is to tell the history of England; and they are to be found— so Mrs. Woolf writes in the foreword to "The Lives of the Obscure" in *The Common Reader* I—in a "faded, out-of-date, obsolete library . . . chiefly subsidized from the shelves of clergymen's widows, and country gentlemen inheriting more books than their wives like to dust." She fancies the readers in such a pleasant local library: the elderly, the marooned, the bored, drifting from newspaper to newspaper, nobody speaking aloud since the room was opened in 1854, and "the obscure sleep on the walls, slouching against each other as if they were too drowsy to stand upright." Why disturb their sleep? She had already disturbed some of them before she wrote this foreword—the Taylors and the Edgeworths, Laetitia Pilkington, Miss Ormerod.[37] Laetitia had left *Memoirs* (Dublin, 1776); material about the Taylors and Edgeworths was drawn from various sources. Obscure people, instead of keeping their identity separate as remarkable people do, "seem to merge into one another, their very boards and title-pages melting into continuous years so that we can lie back and look up into the fine mist-like substance of countless lives, and pass unhindered from century to century, from life to life. Scenes detach themselves." And what scenes Virginia Woolf makes of what are surely only hints! "Let us watch little Miss Frend trotting along the Strand with her father. They meet a man with very bright eyes. 'Mr. Blake,'

37 *London Mercury*, January, 1924; *Nation and Athenaeum*, June, 1923; *Dial*, December, 1924.

says Mr. Frend. It is Mrs. Dyer who pours out tea for them in Clifford's Inn. Mr. Charles Lamb has just left the room. Mrs. Dyer says she married George because his washerwoman cheated him so. What do you think George paid for his shirts, she asks? Gently, beautifully, like the clouds of a balmy evening, obscurity once more traverses the sky, an obscurity that is not empty but thick with the star dust of innumerable lives."

There is Richard Lovell Edgeworth, "the portentous bore," Byron's bore, Day's friend, Maria's father—but delightful to read about in Mrs. Woolf's gleanings from his memoirs. "He brings out, as he bustles and bangs on his way, the diffident, shrinking figures who would otherwise be drowned in darkness ... a series of figures who start up on either side of his progress, mute, astonished, showing us in a way that is even now unmistakable, their amazement at this well-meaning man who bursts in upon them at their studies and interrupts their prayers." There are pitfalls, she admits, in this "nocturnal rambling among forgotten worthies;" it is difficult to keep strictly to the facts and refrain from making scenes that might be found lacking in accuracy. But the history of a character like Thomas Day surpasses the bounds of the credible, and some scenes belong to the abundance of fiction. Think of poor Mrs. Edgeworth's daily life afflicted with Day's inventions—machines that cut turnips, gigantic wheels that ran downhill, machines that climbed walls; and there was an incessant flow of talk about philosophy and nature and M. Rousseau; and he had an enormous appetite which she had to satisfy. It was no use to complain to her husband, who notes that she "lamented about trifles," and asked what she had to complain of—did he ever leave her alone? We remember her life to the last scene of her return from France on the Dover packet, escorted by Mr. Day, who was a ridiculous figure and yet somehow humane, and so she determined never to laugh at him again. "But men were strange; life was difficult; and with a sigh of bewilderment, perhaps of relief, poor Mrs. Edgeworth landed at Dover, was brought to bed of a daughter and died."

Many obscure lives connected in some way with Edgeworth's are "silhouetted with extreme vividness upon a broad disc of interminable chatter"—Edgeworth's. By contrast, it is upon the lady herself that our attention is focused in *Miss Ormerod*. She was a born naturalist. Left alone as a little girl to amuse herself with some pretty beetles, she sat in her high chair and watched them, seeing some astonishing things which she reported to her father: "I saw one of the grubs fall down and the rest came and ate him." Nonsense, said Mr. Ormerod, and when she insisted, he said, "You are not telling the truth," and Mrs. Ormerod said that little girls must not contradict their fathers. But she had a passion that could not be denied, and she ended up seventy years later as a distinguished entomologist. When she was dying she told her doctor that she had chosen her epitaph: "She introduced Paris Green into England"—and there might be a word or two about the Hessian fly. "It's beginning to rain," said the doctor. "How will your enemies like that, Miss Ormerod?" "Hot or cold, wet or dry, insects always flourish!" cried Miss Ormerod, energetically sitting up in bed.

Laetitia Pilkington, "a cross between Moll Flanders and Lady Ritchie, between a rolling and rollicking woman of the town and a lady of breeding and refinement," is in the "great tradition of English women of letters. It is her duty to entertain; it is her instinct to conceal. Still, though her room near the Royal Exchange is threadbare, and the table is spread with old playbills instead of a cloth, and the butter is served in a shoe, and Mr. Worsdale has used the teapot to fetch small beer that very morning, still she presides, still she entertains. Her language is a trifle coarse, perhaps. But who taught her English? The great Dr. Swift." Do the obscure always have some connection with the great? The page or two sum-

ming up her memories of the great Dean "fall upon the race
of life like beams from a lighthouse." She lived on anecdotes,
memories, scandals, which sprinkled the pages she wrote and
was paid for. An earl's great-granddaughter, she steadily descended in the social scale, and in the eighteenth century
it could be a very picturesque descent; and she ended up in a
debtors' prison. But she had read Shakespeare and known
Swift, and "kept through all the shifts and shades of an
adventurous career a gay spirit, something of a lady's breeding, and the gallantry which, at the end of her short life, led
her to crack her joke and enjoy her duck with death at her
heart and duns at her pillow."

Very different indeed is Selina Trimmer, a governess in the
Cavendish family, who arrived at Devonshire House in 1790,
to find half a dozen children, of whom three had no right to
any surname at all. "Soon it must have dawned upon Trimmer as she sat over her Quaker discourse when her pupils
were in bed that she had taken up her lodging in the abode
of vice. Downstairs there was drinking and gambling; upstairs
there were bastards and mistresses." But she stayed on, however much she had to ponder on as she walked in Hyde Park
with her dubious brood, who treated her as an equal in their
"pagan and classless society." "No more devoted family ex-
isted. The children adored their mother. They were on the
best of terms with one another." From governess she became
confidante, and yet preserved her standards. She lived until
1862. "One can imagine her grown very old and very gaunt,
dwindling out her declining years in discreet obscurity. But
what tales she could have told had she liked." [38]

Among the essays in *The Common Reader* and the posthumous volumes, and the reviews that have not been reprinted, are many that might have been worked into *The*

---

[38] *The Captain's Death Bed*, reprinted from review in *New Statesman and Nation*, "The Letters of Lady Harriet Cavendish," July 6,
1940.

Lives of the Obscure had that idea been carried out. Perhaps
it would not really have been possible to "tell the whole
history of England in one obscure life after another," but
it would have enriched the background of more conventional histories. Sir Leslie Stephen, according to Noel Annan,
wished to "prove that the greatest literature is the best source
for understanding the ideas of an age." Mr. Annan does not
agree: "It is precisely the 'ostensible apologists and assailants,'
the minor writers and pamphleteers, whom we must study
if we are to plot the intellectual configurations of the times"
(Annan, *Leslie Stephen*, p. 272). Would Virginia Woolf
have agreed with her father or with her father's biographer?
But in writing of obscure lives the novelist-critic was less interested in intellectual configurations than in what life was like
—to the half sister of Fanny Burney, to Geraldine Jewsbury,
to Parson Woodforde, to Sterne's Eliza—or even to Arch-
bishop Thomson.

Geraldine Jewsbury is known to us only after she was
twenty-nine, and in the first part of the nineteenth century
a woman of twenty-nine was no longer young—"she had
lived her life or she had missed it." What had happened before that is only darkly hinted at. When she and Jane Carlyle
became friends, she had become not only a mass of emotion
and sensibility, but a clever witty woman "who thought for
herself and hated what she called 'respectability' as much as
Mrs. Carlyle hated what she called 'humbug.'" The friendship had its ups and downs. But "a crooning domestic sound
like the purring of a kitten or the humming of a tea-kettle
seems to rise, as we turn the pages of Mrs. Carlyle's letters, from the intercourse of the two incompatible but
deeply attached women." Geraldine's novels have a significance owing nothing to their heroines, "mouldering on their
perches," but something to the questions and convictions
that "still hurtle past the heads of the stuffed figures." They
are dead, but Geraldine survives, independent, courageous,

absurd, with her views on love, morality, religion, and the relations of the sexes—Geraldine with a cigar between her lips.

James Woodforde was a parson who lived in Norfolk toward the end of the eighteenth century, at what, surely, was a breathing space in human affairs. "For once man is content with his lot; harmony is achieved; his house fits him; a tree is a tree; a chair is a chair; each knows his office and fulfils it. Looking through the eyes of Parson Woodforde, the different lives of men seem orderly and settled. Far away guns roar; a King falls; but the sound is not loud enough to scare the rooks here in Norfolk. The proportions of things are different. The Continent is so distant that it seems a mere blur.... But a magnifying glass is laid upon the fields of Norfolk. Every blade of grass is visible there." Carefully chosen details from the parson's diary bring it all to life; for he filled sixty-eight little books with what he did on Monday and what he had for dinner on Tuesday. He talked with himself. "He was of an equable temper, with only such acerbities and touchinesses as are generally to be found in those who have had a love affair in their youth and remained, as they fancy, unwed because of it." Mrs. Woolf suspects that he was glad to consider the question of marriage shelved once for all so that he could settle down with his niece Nancy at Weston Longueville, "and give himself simply and solely, every day and all day, to the great business of living." And what was life like to the parson? "He lived in every room of the house—in the study he wrote sermons, in the dining-room he ate copiously; he cooked in the kitchen, he played cards in the parlour. And then he took his coat and stick and went coursing his greyhounds in the fields. Year in, year out, the provisioning of the house and its defence against the cold of winter and the drought of summer fell upon him. Like a general he surveyed the seasons and took steps to make his own little camp safe with coal and wood and beef

F

and beer against the enemy. His day thus had to accommo-
date a jumble of incongruous occupations. There is religion
to be served, and the pig to be killed; the sick to be visited
and dinner to be eaten; the dead to be buried and beer to be
brewed; Convocation to be attended and the cow to be
bolused. Life and death, mortality and immortality, jostle
in his pages and make a good mixed marriage of it: '... found
the old gentleman almost at his last gasp. Totally senseless
with rattlings in his Throat. Dinner today boiled beef and
Rabbit rosted.' All is as it should be; life is like that." [39] This
eighteenth-century life looks delightful in retrospect, but
there is a hint or two in the parson's diary that Nancy found
it very dull sometimes. "I can assure you," Mrs. Woolf
imagines Nancy as saying to us, "my life was often intolerably
dull.... There is a great deal of humbug talked of the
eighteenth century. Your delight in old times and old diaries
is half impure. You make up something that never had any
existence. Our sober reality is only a dream to you." But a
nice dream. "It is we who change and perish. Parson Woodforde lives on."

But it was all very different a generation later, in Somer-
setshire, and we cannot think of Parson John Skinner living
on, after that morning in December, 1839, when he took his
gun, "walked into the beech wood near his home and shot
himself dead." He was an unhappy man, though a great
antiquary, whose diaries were published fifty years after his
death. He was sure that his village of Camerton was the
ancient Camalodunum, where the father of Caractacus lived
and where Arthur fought the traitor Modred. But the village
of Camerton in 1822 (when the diary begins) had coal mines
and was no place to indulge in dreams about the quaintness
and amenity of old English rural life. The rector had his
private sorrows, and his losses, "though they served nominally

39 *The Common Reader* II revised from "Life Itself," *New Republic*, Aug. 17, 1927.

to make him love God the better, in practice led him to hate men more." Camalodunum and all the correspondence with other antiquaries, and visits where he met the gentlemen who were examining the antiquities of Wiltshire, were all very necessary to an embittered man "who had daily to encounter Hicks the Overseer and Purnell the magistrate, the brothels, the ale-houses, the Methodists, the dropsies and bad legs of Camerton. Even the floods were mitigated if one could reflect that thus Camalodunum must have looked in the time of the Britons." But in the end life had posed too many unanswerable questions—asked with agonizing repetition in the diary—and he shot himself. [40]

VI

Mrs. Woolf writes of Hazlitt that some of his essays "set out to give us a proof and they end by giving us a picture. We are about to plant our feet upon the solid rock of Q.E.D., and behold the rock turns to quagmire and we are knee-deep in mud and water and flowers." That is often our experience, both disconcerting and exhilarating, with the Uncommon Reader as critic. If we have not been given a proof, we have been given something quite as illuminating —a memorable image. Would it be easy to forget a certain quality of Gibbon's style after this description? Writing about "The Historian and 'The Gibbon,'" she notes that many chapters of *The Decline and Fall* glide away without leaving a trace; "we seem, for hours on end, mounted on a celestial rocking-horse, which, as it gently sways up and down, remains rooted in a single spot." We begin to suspect that his vast fame may be one of "those vague diffusions of acquiescence." This style is singularly open to imitation, well adapted to invest little ideas with large bodies. "And then we

40 *The Common Reader* II.

turn to the book again and to our amazement we find the rocking-horse has left the ground; we are mounted on a winged steed; we are sweeping in wide circles through the air and below us Europe unfolds; the ages change and pass; a miracle has taken place." [41] Gilbert White, that "very fine specimen of the eighteenth century clerical naturalist," is transformed by her imagination when she tries to find the man behind the vegetable and animal world of Selborne. There is no portrait of him, he has no face, he escapes identification. But at times he raises his eyes from the insect in the grass, and looks, and listens. In that moment he escapes from Selborne and "comes winging his way to us in the dusk along the hedgerows. A clerical owl? A parson with the wings of a bird? A hybrid? But his own description fits him best. 'The kestrel or wind-hover,' he says, 'has a peculiar mode of hanging in the air in one place, his wings all the time being briskly agitated.' " [42]

In an essay on Virginia Woolf as critic, Louis Kronenberger writes that she "nowhere altered the face of criticism, as she did the face of the novel." [43] That she might have done so, had she not always given first place to her fiction, is surely suggested by the many fruitful ideas in her essays, whether we choose to call these essays "critical" or merely "literary." She was not a systematic critic, as David Daiches and others have said. [44] She did not have a system; only a sensibility. Mr. Kronenberger grants her a "superb responsiveness" to literature. Little systems have their day and make their often valuable contributions to a critical tradition. But the superbly responsive critic, with a style admirably fitted to express that responsiveness, is much more rare than a critic with a system. Mrs. Woolf had critical methods,

41 *The Death of the Moth, and Other Essays.*
42 "White's Selborne" in *The Captain's Death Bed.*
43 *The Republic of Letters: Essays on Various Writers* (New York, 1955).
44 David Daiches, *Virginia Woolf* (New Directions Books, 1942).

which she used with exquisite discrimination, according to the subject she was writing about. She never lost sight of the "book itself" when its special quality was in question. But she adopted various approaches, undisturbed by the risk of committing some of the fallacies so diligently damned from time to time by one school or another of criticism: the biographical, historical, sociological, psychological, affective, intentional, and the rest of them. Leslie Stephen, a disciple of Matthew Arnold, conceived the critic's role to be that of a judge; a judge of moral content within the context of literature as a criticism of life. His daughter did not. But they were in agreement on some points. Leslie Stephen, writes Noel Annan, "warned the 'pure' critics that to wrench a poem or novel from its social setting is to neglect the fact that a work of art has a life of its own in Time, and is subject to different kinds of perception in each age, in that the communication between author and reader is constantly changing." [45]

There is no end to the diversity of critical theories. Mr. Annan, in Chapter IX of his biography of Leslie Stephen, imagines an entertaining symposium of critics past and present, from Dr. Johnson to Dr. Leavis, who start out by discussing Stephen's contribution. Stephen listens and is much perplexed. Among other points of view is that of the Bloomsbury group. "Though we speak as a bloc," says their spokesman, "we are, of course, creatures of diverse views and, recognising this to be so, we appeal to the great Romantic principle of Diversity. . . . No critic can be infallible or impartial: his judgments proceed from a personal vision of artistic and moral excellence. Why, then, spin webs of orthodoxy, why lay down elaborate critical canons?" If this is true of the critic, it is much more so of the artist. "Is not every work of art," pleads Virginia Woolf, "born of an original imagination and ought not the critic to concern himself

45 Noel Annan, *Leslie Stephen*, pp. 272–73.

with the creative act, the birth-pangs, the struggle of the artist to solve certain technical problems? The critic's duty is to communicate to the reader the particular vision of the artist, not to award good and bad conduct marks." And so the argument goes on, enlightening but inconclusive.

In her essay on Hazlitt, Mrs. Woolf characterizes one of his opinions as "initiatory and inspiring rather than conclusive and complete," but adds, "there is something to be said for the critic who starts the reader on a journey and fires him with a phrase to shoot off on adventures of his own." [46] She herself often does just that. She also again and again communicates to her readers the excitement of her own voyages and discoveries. "To illumine, to make visible and desirable"—what she said was the aim of Edmund Gosse is her own achievement. [47]

46 "William Hazlitt," in *The Common Reader* II.
47 "Edmund Gosse," in *The Moment, and Other Essays*.

3. Fiction

Shaping the Globe

I

IF WE LOOK over Virginia Woolf's shoulder to discover her perspective as a novelist we see in the foreground nothing so prosaic as Defoe's earthenware pot or so metaphysical as the Soul—Russian or otherwise. But a Globe, a recurrent image in both her *Diary* and her novels, might stand there as a symbol of her pursuit of "Mrs. Brown"—the spirit we live by, Life itself. Mrs. Woolf herself was wary of symbols. Completing the most "inner" and symbolic of her novels, *The Waves*, she noted in her *Diary* (Feb. 7, 1931): "What interests me in the last stage was the freedom and boldness with which my imagination picked up, used and tossed aside all the images, symbols which I had prepared. I am sure that this is the right way of using them—not in set pieces, as I had tried at first, coherently, but simply as images, never making them work out; only suggest." The globe is life: "I ask myself sometimes whether one is not hypnotised, as a child by a silver globe, by life; and whether this is living. . . . I should like to take the globe in my hands and feel it quietly, round, smooth, heavy, and so hold it, day after day" (*Diary*, Nov. 28, 1928).

Several of Mrs. Woolf's leading characters take this globe in their hands at some stage in their experience of life. Katharine Hilbery, in the last chapter of *Night and Day*, "held in her hands for one brief moment the globe which we spend our lives in trying to shape, round, whole, and entire, from the confusion of chaos." Bernard, at the end of *The Waves*, reflecting upon the lives of his six friends and trying to come to terms with life, thinks of life as a globe which we turn about in our fingers: "the crystal, the globe of life as one calls it, far from being hard and cold to the touch, has walls of the thinnest air. If I press them, all will burst." Eleanor in *The Years*, at the end of the party and the book, as she sits meditating, hollowed her hands in her lap: "she felt that she wanted to enclose the present moment; to make it stay; to fill it fuller and fuller, with the past, the present, and the future, until it shone, whole, bright, deep with understanding." Lily Briscoe, in the final section of *To the Lighthouse*, tries to express what Mrs. Ramsay had made of the house and the people and the island: "There might be lovers, whose gift it was to choose out the elements of things and place them together and so, giving them a wholeness not theirs in life, make of some scene, or meeting of peoples (all now gone and separate), one of those globed compacted things over which thought lingers and love plays."

This globe, life—what is it? According to one definition, in terms which Mrs. Woolf would never have used, it is the interaction of the organism with the environment. Or, in her terms, the interplay between the inner and the outer, the Internal and the External, the individual and "life in general," Night and Day. Her heroine Katharine Hilbery meditates: "Why should there be this perpetual disparity between the thought and the action, between the life of solitude and the life of society, this astonishing precipice on one side of which the soul was active and in broad daylight, on the other side of which it was contemplative and dark as night?" Or take the inner and the outer in Mrs. Ramsay's relation to life: "a sort of transaction went on between them, in which she was on one side and life was on another, and she was always trying to get the better of it, as it was of her; and sometimes they parleyed (when she sat alone); there were, she remembered, great reconciliation scenes." Are these reconciliation scenes the *moments,* when inner and outer, the Self and the Not-Self, are in brief harmony? It had dawned upon Mrs. Woolf, while working on *The Years,* that the discovery of that book was "the combination of the external and the internal." In the *Diary* (Nov. 28, 1928), she asks herself: "What is my own position towards the inner and the outer?" Some combination should be possible, eliminating all waste, deadness, superfluity; "to give the moment whole; whatever it includes. Say that the moment is a combination of thought; sensation; the voice of the sea." The moment is not just a fleeting revelation, "a match burning in a crocus, an inner meaning almost expressed," such as Clarissa Dalloway experiences. Many of these fleeting revelations may come before we feel the globe in our hands.

It is best to follow Mrs. Woolf's own way with symbols— not making them work out, only suggest; and not worry too much over the boundary line between the individual consciousness and what lies outside. She herself shifted the boundaries as she proceeded from *Jacob's Room* to *Between the Acts.* It is clear from her *Diary* that each new novel presented afresh the challenge to her art: how to keep the delicate balance between the inner and the outer; how to throw out all that was inessential in the stream of consciousness as well as in the stream of events; and how to bring about in the experience of her leading characters the revelatory moments of harmony—however fleeting. "Life in general," a favorite phrase, seems at times to mean the outer aspect of things. "The interest in life," she wrote in an essay, "does not lie in what people do, nor even in their relations to each other, but largely in the power to communicate with a third party, antagonistic, enigmatic, yet perhaps persuadable, which one may call life in general." [1] So Mrs. Ramsay, in her transactions with life, experiences rare moments of reconciliation. So Sterne, through a certain quality of style, a touch on the visual sense, brings "an alteration in the movement of the mind which makes it pause and widen its gaze and slightly change its attention. We are looking out at life in general." [2] So Turgenev turns our eyes away from the intimate drawing-room scene, to look out the window at the moonlit garden—and life in general.

But how keep "life in general" in Mrs. Woolf's novels from being only a vague abstraction? It is her gift for conveying the concrete image that is brilliantly effective in making us imagine the External. Her friend Lowes Dickinson, as she notes in her *Diary*, December 28, 1935, "never notices a face or a cat or a dog or a flower, except in the flow of the universal." Mrs. Woolf notices everything in the flow of the particular, and from the store of images in her memory, selects those most relevant to her artistic purpose. All of her senses are alert. She loved, E. M. Forster recalls in his Rede Lecture (May, 1941), receiving sensations— "sights, sounds, tastes—passing them through her mind, where they encountered theories, memories, and then bringing them out again, through a pen, on to a bit of paper." "In the strictest sense of the word," wrote Clive Bell (*Old Friends*), "she is a seer. More often than not her creative impulses spring from her sense of a scene." She had a "pure painterlike vision." She does not become, like D. H. Lawrence, one with Nature. Nature is always part of the External, whether seen through the eyes of her characters or existing in its own right, apart from human beings. Hers is a comprehensive vision, including the moth and the snail as well as the clouds and the stars, the changing aspects of sea and moor and river, country

1 "On Not Knowing French," *New Republic*, Feb. 13, 1929.
2 *Granite and Rainbow*, p. 136.

gardens and city parks. And the External also comprises the streets and buildings and bridges, the country houses and college chapels, the Reading Room of the British Museum, the churches in the Strand, the restaurants in Soho and in the City, the shops in Bond Street—all the places where people are to be found—the anonymous people who are outside the intimate relationships in which the Self can be lost. One is aware of the flow of human life even in that most inner of the novels, *The Waves. The Voyage Out, Night and Day, Jacob's Room, Mrs. Dalloway*—though not *To the Lighthouse—The Years, Between the Acts,* even the fantastic *Orlando*—all give the impression of a well-peopled world. Much of the impression is created by London with its streets and buses and passing throngs; passing not only through the streets during the moment of time of the Dalloways and Hilberys and Pargiters, but also through the centuries of the life of the great city. The crowds crossing Waterloo Bridge from the Surrey side to the Strand and from the Strand to the Surrey side—has this procession gone on forever? But what of the individuals who have an inner life, for whom these crowds are a part of the outer flow of events?— Katharine Hilbery and Ralph, riding on the top of the bus through the night streets, aware of the unknown life behind the lighted windows; Mary Datchet mingling with the workaday crowds along the Strand or Southampton Row; Jacob on the bus carrying him along Oxford Street to his job in the City; Mrs. Dalloway buying roses in Bond Street on a June morning; Peter Walsh on his long jaunt through the evening crowds between Russell Square and Westminster; Orlando sailing up the busy Thames (as a woman) and seeking adventure in Soho and Leicester Square (as a man); Sally and Martin stepping on and off the pavement, threading their way through the noon crowds in Fleet Street; even Jinny in *The Waves* standing for a moment in the Tube in the heart of London, feeling the rush of wheels and the

press of feet above her head, or Bernard stepping off the
platform at Euston Station, hearing the roar of the traffic and
aware of the "passage of undifferentiated faces, feeling his
individual self about to be submerged," and even Flush,
shopping with his mistress, smelling his way along Wimpole
Street, assaulted by the whole battery of smells that lay beyond the range of the human nose.

II

A writer's first novel is likely to be "an unguarded one,
where the author displays his gifts, without knowing how to
dispose of them to the best advantage." [3] Mrs. Woolf is
speaking of Meredith's *Richard Feverel*; it is equally true of
her own first novel, *The Voyage Out*. She explained in a
letter to Lytton Strachey (Feb. 28, 1916) what she had
wished to do: "to give the feeling of a vast tumult of life, as
various and disorderly as possible, which should be cut short
for a moment by the death, and go on again—and the
whole was to have a sort of pattern, and be somehow controlled. The difficulty was to keep any sort of coherence,—
also to give enough detail to make the characters interesting
—which Forster says I didn't do." Strachey read it with
"breathless pleasure," but felt at the end as if "it was really
only the beginning of an enormous novel, which had been
almost accidentally cut short by the death of Rachel." It
lacked the "cohesion of a dominating idea"; but he found
something Tolstoyan in the account of Rachel's illness,
something of the eighteenth century in "the absence of
folly," and it was "very, very unvictorian!" (Letter of Feb. 25,
1916.) By "unvictorian" Strachey may have meant a certain
cool detachment, an unsentimental handling of romantic
love, a concern with intelligence as at least equally important
with goodness, and a frank expression of the agnostic view-

3 "The Novels of George Meredith," *The Common Reader* II.

point in religion. Strachey found the chapel scene the "best *morceau* of all." And it is indeed quite a morceau: a Sunday service held in the resort hotel, in the old chapel of the monks, to which Rachel dutifully goes with the other conventionally minded guests. But she gives it a close attention that is not conventional. Coming out after the service into the hall—where the little band of worshipers is greeted with respectful glances by those who had not gone to church, "although their clothing made it clear that they approved of Sunday to the very verge of going to church"—Rachel is asked by her aunt, "Did you go to church?" "Yes," said Rachel. "For the last time," she added.

Mrs. Woolf had completed the novel in July, 1913. Rereading it for the first time nearly seven years later, she noted in her *Diary* (Feb. 4, 1920) that it is "an assortment of patches —here simple and severe—here frivolous and shallow—here like God's truth—here strong and free flowing as I could wish.... The failures are ghastly enough to make my cheeks burn—and then a turn of a sentence, a direct look ahead of me, makes them burn in a different way." She felt that "the young woman" had quite a gift for pen and ink, and took her fences gallantly, but would go down to posterity "the author of cheap witticisms, smart satires, and even, I find, vulgarisms—crudities rather." But she understands how people might prefer it to *Night and Day*, finding it a more gallant and inspiring spectacle.

The theme of *The Voyage Out* is the awakening of Rachel Vinrace, undeveloped and immature at twenty-four, feeling nothing deeply except her music, which expresses all that so far she is interested in expressing. Motherless, she has been brought up by maiden aunts in nunlike seclusion in Richmond. The people around her are little more than symbols— of age, of motherhood, of learning; and she cares little about connecting with them. "To feel anything strongly was to create an abyss between herself and others, who feel strongly perhaps, but differently.... It was far better to play the piano and forget the rest." Many weeks later she is asked by Terence, who sees her looking meditatively at a group of fellow picnickers near her, "What are you looking at?" "She was a little startled, but answered directly, 'Human beings.' " In awareness of life she has come quite a long way from the girl who started on a voyage on her father's ship, a cargo ship going to South American ports, with her uncle and aunt, Ridley and Helen Ambrose, whom she scarcely knows, and several other passengers; among them a Greek scholar and—for part of the way—Mr. and Mrs. Dalloway. Mr. Dalloway, a rising young politician, yielding one day to a casual impulse, kisses Rachel. That surprising experience and the discussion of it with her aunt mark a stage in her coming alive. People are ceasing to be symbols. Her aunt notices a change in her and begins to draw her out in a humorous, detached way, and to suggest to her that she might become a person on her own account. "The vision of her own personality, of herself as a real everlasting thing, different from anything else, unmergeable, like the sea or the wind, flashed into Rachel's mind, and she became profoundly excited at the thought of living."

Rachel stays for many weeks with her uncle and aunt at a seaside villa near a resort somewhere in South America, while her father pursues his business affairs farther down the coast. Near the villa is a hotel, reconditioned from an old monastery, with a shifting group of guests, mostly English, some of whom we come to know very well. There is a dance at the hotel, a picnic on the mountain, and a five-day trip up the river in a small launch, through an exotic tropical landscape—almost word for word, as Winifred Holtby points out, described by Sir Walter Raleigh in his *Discovery of Guiana*. On the trip Rachel and Terence Hewet, who have been reluctantly falling in love, become engaged. Rachel has been wondering for some time what it means to be in love.

Walking by herself one day, with a volume of Gibbon in one hand and a novel by Balzac in the other, contributions to her education, at her naïve request, by her uncle and Terence's Cambridge friend, she sits down on the grass to reflect. "For some time she observed a great yellow butterfly, which was opening and closing its wings very slowly on a little flat stone. 'What is it to be in love?' she demanded after a long silence; each word as it came into being seemed to shove itself out into an unknown sea. Hypnotised by the wings of the butterfly, and awed by the discovery of a terrible possibility in life, she sat for some time longer."

Everybody at the hotel is pleased by the engagement—the second that has taken place in the group—and the atmosphere becomes quite gay. Terence and Rachel talk of their future life: where they will live in London, what they will do, the walks they will take; we seem to be sharing a long married life. Then, disaster. Rachel contracts a fever and dies. (One remembers that Thoby Stephen died suddenly of typhoid fever on a holiday in Greece.) The "voyage out" takes on tragic significance: the literal voyage out to South America, the voyaging out of Rachel's adventuring personality, and the voyage out of life altogether.

This first novel is in many ways traditional, with its chronological sequence, easily followed flashbacks, central characters fully drawn and others receding into the background, a narrative diversified with scenes and dialogue, explanations of what goes on in people's minds, but not in stream-of-consciousness technique, description of settings, and so on. And the world of the novel is pre-1914 England: distinct classes, a politics of progress, awareness of the Empire, a leisurely atmosphere. Mr. Dalloway has ideals, conservative ideals, and is proud of his efforts to improve conditions. He believes in Unity—"Unity of aim, of dominion, of progress. The dispersion of the best ideas over the greatest area." Rachel asks questions and is informed that the English "seem, on the

whole, whiter than most men, and their records cleaner." But
of course unmentionable things are done even in our midst.
"Have you ever been in a factory, Miss Vinrace?—No, I suppose not—I may say I hope not." Rachel had almost never
walked through a poor street. But it is owing to Mr. Dalloway that thousands of girls in Lancashire can spend an
hour in the open air that their mothers spent at the looms.
Statistics and masses do not impress Rachel, who pictures to
herself some old widow who, because of Mr. Dalloway's
efforts, may have a little more tea and a few more lumps of
sugar in her cupboard, but who may be gazing out her window longing for someone to talk to. Mr. Dalloway says that
he has never met a woman who knew what was meant by
statesmanship; and he answers Rachel's naïve arguments by
political clichés—"I understand you to mean that the whole
of modern society is based upon cooperative effort." Their
attempt at communication is a failure. Rachel is haunted by
the idea that "if one went back far enough, everything perhaps was intelligible; everything was in common; for the
mammoths who pastured in the fields of Richmond High
Street had turned into paving stones and boxes full of rib-
bon, and her aunts." Mammoths have a way of intruding
into Mrs. Woolf's world, as a symbol of the flow of time.

Clarissa Dalloway—the young matron, not yet the rather
tired fifty-year-old hostess—plays a good second to her husband. She thinks of England, especially here at sea on the
ship, and of what it means to be English. "One thinks of all
we've done, and our navies, and the people in India and
Africa, and how we've gone on century after century, sending
out boys from little country villages—and of men like you,
Dick, and it makes one feel as if one couldn't bear *not* to be
English! Think of the light burning over the House, Dick!
When I stood on deck just now I seemed to see it. It's what
one means by London."

The two young Cambridge men obviously owe much to

Virginia Woolf's knowledge, through her father and brothers and friends, of what such young men are like. Mrs. Ambrose, whose husband is a scholar, can be quite caustic about their characteristics. One of the most interesting relationships in the novel develops between Mrs. Ambrose and the ugly and arrogant but brilliant St. John Hirst, who is trying to decide whether to choose the Bar or be a university don. Some undercurrent of sympathy runs between them. He is more interesting than Terence, who is charming but indolent, vaguely planning to write novels and taking his time about it because he has a small inherited income. He develops through his relationship with Rachel, and they experience happiness as they talk quietly together about ordinary things: "Very gently and quietly, almost as if it were the blood singing in her veins, or the water of the stream running over stones, Rachel became conscious of a new feeling within her. She wondered for a moment what it was, and then said to herself, with a little surprise at recognizing in her own person so famous a thing: 'This is happiness, I suppose.' And aloud to Terence she spoke, 'This is happiness.' On the heels of her words he answered, 'This is happiness,' upon which they guessed that the feeling had sprung in both of them at the same time. They began therefore to describe how this felt and that felt, how like it was and yet how different; for they were very different."

Both young men meet the ordeal of Rachel's illness in a way that brings out their finest qualities. That illness is handled—as experienced by Rachel herself—through the fevered imaginings of her delirium, in a completely convincing way. Never again does Mrs. Woolf so describe illness and death; and for this achievement alone the novel would be memorable. It is typical of Mrs. Woolf's indifference to plot that the reason Rachel fell victim to the fever—whether the vegetables were not washed properly at the villa or whether she caught the infection during the expedition up the river—is never made clear. But the root of the disaster is precisely its meaninglessness. Recent happenings are used effectively in the nightmares of Rachel's illness. During one of the moments when Terence is sitting by her bedside hoping for a moment of lucidity, he kisses her and she opens her eyes. "But she saw only an old woman slicing a man's head off with a knife. 'There it falls!' she murmured." Some weeks before, as she was exploring the corridors of the hotel, she looked out a back window upon the kitchen quarters and saw an old native woman cutting off the heads of chickens for dinner. The sheltered Rachel's mind registers the scene with ugly vividness. She is tormented in her delirium by faces forcing themselves close to her and by sights connected with some plot, some adventure, some escape. Just when the climax is at hand, something slips in her brain and the effort to understand begins all over again. "At last the faces went further away; she fell into a deep pool of sticky water, which eventually closed over her head. She saw nothing and heard nothing but a faint booming sound, which was the sound of the sea rolling over her head. While all her tormentors thought she was dead, she was not dead, but curled up at the bottom of the sea. There she lay, sometimes seeing darkness, sometimes light, while every now and then some one turned her over at the bottom of the sea."

Terence's pain during this long agonizing suspense was a revelation to him. "He had never realized before that underneath every action, underneath the life of every day, pain lies, quiescent, but ready to devour; he seemed to be able to see suffering, as if it were a fire, curling up over the edges of all action, eating away the lives of men and women." He stood looking out the window at the scattered lights of the town beneath, thinking of the newly engaged couple at the hotel— pleasant ordinary people—and how they were "venturing out unwittingly and by their happiness laying themselves open to suffering such as this. How did they dare to love each other ... how had he himself dared to live as he had lived, rapidly and carelessly, passing from one thing to another, loving Rachel as he had loved her? Never again would he feel secure; he would never believe in the stability of life, or forget what depths of pain lie beneath small happiness and feelings of content and safety." Then comes one of those shifts of perspective and Terence looks out at life in general. "The light of his candle flickered over the boughs of a tree outside the window, and as the branch swayed in the darkness there came before his mind a picture of all the world that lay outside his window; he thought of the immense river and the immense forest, the vast stretches of dry earth and the plains of the sea that encircled the earth; from the sea the sky rose steep and enormous, and the air washed profoundly between the sky and the sea. How vast and dark it must be tonight, lying exposed to the wind; and in all this great space it was curious to think how few the towns were, and how like little rings of light they were, scattered here and there among the swelling uncultivated folds of the world. And in these towns were little men and women, tiny men and women." What, he thinks, did anything matter?

A few days later Terence and St. John, waiting in the drawing room, are forced to listen to Ridley Ambrose, restless and unable to work, pacing up and down, reciting poetry in an undertone; as he had done along the Embankment just before he and Helen boarded their steamer, and as he does later in the day, pacing up and down along the terrace, reciting:

> Peor and Baalim
> Forsake their Temples dim....

Strangely discomforting sounds to the young men. (So, in *To the Lighthouse*, Mr. Ramsay paces up and down, reciting scraps of poetry—a habit, no doubt, of Sir Leslie Stephen's.

He always recited Milton's *Ode on the Nativity* on Christmas Night.) [4]

Terence, called to Rachel's bedside by the doctor, finds her conscious and calm. She smiles at him and says "Hullo," and he replies—"It has been wretched without you." "The longer he sat there the more profoundly was he conscious of the peace invading every corner of his soul." And when she ceases to breathe, "it was happiness.... They had now what they had always wanted to have, the union which had been impossible while they lived. Unconscious whether he thought the words or spoke them aloud, he said, 'No two people have ever been so happy as we have been. No one has ever loved as we have loved.'" The brief closing of this scene is as moving as anything Virginia Woolf ever wrote, and as true to experience. The beautiful "moment" is of brief duration, but brief as it is, it is one of those moments of illumination that happen in her world. Then: "As he saw the passage outside the room, and the table with the cups and the plates, it suddenly came over him that here was a world in which he would never see Rachel again."

The currents of life swirl around this disastrous cutting-off of promise, of youth and happiness, and flow on again.

"In my own opinion," wrote Mrs. Woolf in her *Diary*, March 27, 1919, "*N&D* is a much more mature and finished and satisfactory book than *The Voyage Out*; as it has reason to be. I suppose I lay myself open to the charge of niggling with emotions that don't really matter.... L. finds the philosophy very melancholy.... Yet, if one is to deal with people on a large scale and say what one thinks, how can one avoid melancholy? I don't admit to being hopeless though: only the spectacle is a profoundly strange one; and as the current answers don't do, one has to grope for a new one, and the process of discarding the old, when one is by no

4 F. W. Maitland, *Life and Letters of Leslie Stephen* (London: Duckworth & Co., 1906).

means certain what to put in their place, is a sad one." The problem seems to be mainly *what* to say, not, as later, *how* to say it. *Night and Day* appeared in October, 1919. E. M. Forster, whose criticism she respected, called it a strictly formal and classical work, and thought such a work required "a greater degree of lovability in the characters" than a book like *The Voyage Out*, which was "more vague and universal"; and he didn't find any of the characters lovable. Katherine Mansfield compared her to Jane Austen—a comparison that did not please her, though it was certainly invited by the pattern of the book. A matrimonial theme is worked out with three female and two male characters, all young and variously in love, ending with two marriages and one lady left out. The time covered is a few months in London, with an interlude in Lincolnshire, and the atmosphere is that of Edwardian social comedy. The love affairs develop in a leisurely fashion: Rodney first with Katharine, then with Cassandra—the Lincolnshire cousin who comes to town in the nick of time to console Rodney; Katharine first with Rodney and then with Ralph; and Mary first with Ralph and then with no one; and all of them meeting, parting, regrouping, changing partners. Jane Austen could have handled this choreography more briskly and neatly and entertainingly than Mrs. Woolf, who, nevertheless, suggests, without quite expressing, a greater depth of emotion and of psychological complexity in the relationships.

In this Edwardian world before 1914 the young men study law or write novels or plays or scholarly papers—if they have incomes and leisure; the young women are firmly anchored in good families, in town or country, though a few, like Mary Datchet, are beginning to develop careers and work for causes, such as woman suffrage. Parents and relatives and connections of one sort or another give an impression of a closely knit society. The class structure is still clearly marked, and a class difference complicates the love affair of Ralph Denham, who lives in Highgate with his small-income middle-class family, and Katharine Hilbery, who belongs to the intellectual aristocracy and lives in Chelsea. The review of *Night and Day* in the *Times Literary Supplement* pointed out the geographical significance: "Highgate has come to Chelsea; raw strength to exquisite tradition." The Empire is still furnishing outdoor relief to the ruling classes. But Katharine's cousins, the Otways, are finding it difficult to keep up their old Lincolnshire estate on a retired Indian officer's pension, which has to provide education for ten children. Cassandra Otway, a younger daughter, makes her room a breeding place for silkworms; in such families there are always one or two daughters at home, "nursing sick animals, tending silk-worms, or playing the flute in their bedrooms." And in such houses they play "the great make-believe game of social life," intended for people like Lady Otway. Mrs. Woolf devotes Chapter XVII to the social system of the Otways, with whom Katharine is staying, while trying to make up her mind about love and marriage. She listens to the talk of the elderly ladies and learns that "to be engaged to marry someone with whom you are not in love is an inevitable step in a world where the existence of passion is only a traveler's story brought from the heart of deep forests and told so rarely that wise people doubt whether the story can be true." It is through Mary Datchet that Katharine at last perceives that passion is not just a traveler's story.

The relationship between Katharine and Mary—both of them in love with Ralph, though Katharine is confused about her own emotions—is one of the most interesting in the novel, and the scenes between them are handled with insight and originality. Mary has suffered one of the major defeats of the emotional life, loving deeply where the love is not returned. She could have married Ralph; she prefers to help Katharine to an understanding of both herself and Ralph. Katharine is bewildered by Mary, but finally enlightened.

Mary values truth even when to perceive it means her own disaster. "That's how it feels then," thinks Katharine; and then says, "You've got that." And Mary replies, "Yes. . . . One wouldn't *not* be in love." After Mary has given up Ralph, she takes stock of her life during a long walk through the crowded streets, gradually passing from an acute sense of herself as an individual to something like a vision of the scheme of things. "It only needed a persistent effort of thought, stimulated in this strange way by the crowd and the noise, to climb the crest of existence and see it all laid out once and for ever. . . . Not happiness"—the words escaped her as she sat down on a bench along the Embankment. "To her they represented the rare flower or splinter of rock brought down by a climber in proof that he has stood for a moment, at least, upon the highest peak of the mountain." Her experience was a "curious transformation from the particular to the universal." Her post in the future, with the solace of work, would be in "one of those exposed and desolate stations shunned naturally by happy people." That work of hers is made credible to us, and she herself does not idealize it. "Having lost what is best," she thinks, "I do not mean to pretend that any other view does instead."

Mary's devotion to the Cause is honest in a way not like that of her co-worker, Mrs. Seal, who is handled with a satirical touch. Mrs. Seal finds it difficult to believe that people cannot see the truth that the cause of women is the cause of humanity—because it is all so *simple*, really! "She referred to a matter that was a perpetual source of bewilderment to her—the extraordinary incapacity of the human race, in a world where the good is so unmistakably divided from the bad, of distinguishing one from the other, and embodying what ought to be done in a few large, simple Acts of Parliament, which would, in a very short time, completely change the lot of humanity." Feminist though she was, Virginia Woolf never cherished such illusions.

Mary has discovered that there are different ways of loving, and so has Katharine; and a surprising number of such discoveries are made in Mrs. Woolf's novels, up to the very last one, *Between the Acts*, where the relationship between the old brother and sister is beautifully depicted. It is also surprising that after the first two novels young courting couples like Terence and Rachel in *The Voyage Out* and the two successful pairs in *Night and Day* play relatively minor roles. But there are varieties of married love, both in the earlier and in the later years; deep family affections; illicit and casual loves, like Jacob's affair with Florinda; the love of comrades, sometimes homosexual; and the intricate group relationship of the six in *The Waves* with Perceval, the figure in the center. The search for that which unites, for that which connects, and so mitigates the isolation of the individual human being, is never ending. There are moments of union when the globe shapes itself, and rare moments when through the quality of one person a whole group of diverse individuals is briefly drawn into a magic circle—as around Mrs. Ramsay's dinner table.

Perhaps following the course of the love affairs in *Night and Day* began to bore Mrs. Woolf a little. Certainly they are rather long drawn out, diversified though they are by pleasant group excursions to Kew Gardens and Hampton Court and Greenwich. Katharine and Ralph create an embarrassing situation by refusing to be officially engaged, keeping Mr. and Mrs. Hilbery in ignorance, and Rodney and Cassandra in suspense. But the situation brings out the character of Mrs. Hilbery, and, Mr. Forster to the contrary, she is a lovable person. She has an amusing mind, which goes off at tangents and juxtaposes irrelevancies in the manner of Elizabeth Bennett's mother, though she is never silly. Her way of dealing with her daughter's puzzling behavior is in amusing contrast with that of Mr. Hilbery, who tries to approach the problem rationally and to assert his fatherly authority, and who gets nowhere.[5] Mrs. Hilbery's way is devious and intuitive and successful. A little earlier, when both Rodney and Ralph are in the running, Mrs. Hilbery remarks, "It's very dull that you can marry only one husband.... I always wish that you could marry anybody who wants to marry you. Perhaps they'll come to that in time." Now, with only Ralph in the picture, Katharine declares that she is not in love. But her mother leads her on to talking about Ralph, listens, and "seemed to draw her conclusions rather by looking at her daughter than by listening to her, and, if crossexamined, she would probably have given a highly inaccurate version of Ralph Denham's life-history, except that he was penniless, fatherless, and lived at Highgate—all of which was much in his favour. But by means of these furtive glances she had assured herself that Katharine was in a state which gave her, alternately, the most exquisite pleasure and the most profound alarm." Mrs. Hilbery ejaculates at last, "It's all done in five minutes at a Registry Office nowadays, if you think the Church service a little florid—which it is, though there are noble things in it." But Katharine declares that they don't want to be married. Couldn't they live together without being married? This is a shock—it is a pre-1914 society—but Mrs. Hilbery absorbs it and merely asks carefully, "Does that grave young man ask it of you?" "Oh, no," replies Katharine, "neither of us asks anything." Mrs. Hilbery wonders aloud whether she can help by recalling what she herself had once felt. Her eyes growing blank, she "peered down the enormously long corridor of days at the far end of which the little figures of herself and her husband appeared fantastically attired, clasping hands upon a moonlit beach, with roses swinging in the dusk." They were going in a little boat out to a ship at night. Katharine, soothed, imagines it all—the enormous space of the sea, the voyage over the green and purple

5 Noel Annan (*Leslie Stephen*) calls Mr. Hilbery a "complementary portrait" of Leslie Stephen, p. 301, fn.

waters, her mother "that ancient voyager." Mrs. Hilbery continues her reverie aloud, beyond the personal to the general—who knows where we are bound for or who has sent us or why, who knows anything? "And the soft sound beating through the dim words was heard by her daughter as the breaking of waves solemnly in order upon the vast shore that she gazed upon."

In the end Ralph and Katharine become one in spirit, and walk by the river at night, entering that enchanted region where "she might speak to him, but with that strange tremor in his voice, those eyes blindly adoring, whom did he answer? what woman did he see? And where was she walking, and who was her companion? Moments, fragments, a second of vision, and then the flying waters, dissipating and dissolving; then, too, the recollection from chaos, the return of security, the earth firm, superb and brilliant in the sun. From the heart of his darkness he spoke his thanksgiving; from a region as far, as hidden, she answered him. . . . Pausing, they looked down into the river which bore its dark tide of waters, endlessly moving, beneath them." Turning back, they found themselves opposite Katharine's home, with its friendly lamps burning.

So Ralph and Katharine set out on their marriage venture, like Darcy and Elizabeth Bennett, but one feels more confident about the future of Jane Austen's couple than about Virginia Woolf's. Both the psychology and the social order of 1810 seem more secure.

III

Night and Day is an imperfect but delightful novel; with its echoes of Jane Austen and even of George Eliot, it is still authentic Virginia Woolf. Yet neither of her first two novels places her among the creators of the "modern" novel. The novel became "modern" chiefly because of the work of Joyce,

Conrad, Lawrence, and Woolf, whose later novels broke the mold of her earlier. Few critics would seriously dispute the preeminence of these four, though they might have favorites for the top place. An article in the *TLS* (Jan. 13, 1961), referring especially to Mrs. Woolf, calls attention to the "temporal gap between, say, *Middlemarch* and *To the Lighthouse*." It was the search to find the form to express her own vision of life that pushed her into experimentation, and continued to prevent her from doing what lesser novelists have done—go on, after a success, to repeat the formula. In her *Diary* (July 27, 1934) she noted: "I have to some extent forced myself to break every mould and find a fresh form of being, that is of expression, for everything I feel and think. ... But this needs constant effort." *The Mark on the Wall* (1917) was the earliest of the experimental pieces to be published; *Kew Gardens* (1919) came next; then *An Unwritten Novel* (1920). These three, together with several other sketches, make up the collection *Monday or Tuesday*, published by the Hogarth Press in 1921. They were in her mind when she began to think of a form for a new novel: "conceive (?) *Mark on the Wall, K.G.* and *Unwritten Novel* taking hands and dancing in unity. What the unity shall be I have yet to discover; the theme is a blank to me; but I see immense possibilities in the form I hit upon more or less by chance two weeks ago" (*Diary*, Jan. 26, 1920).

The Mark on the Wall plays with the stream-of-consciousness technique in a pattern of reverie intermittently focused on a mark above the fireplace. The daydreamer before the fire wonders what the mark is; drifts off into a free association of ideas and images, cuts the reverie short and looks again at the mark, drifts off again, and so on till interrupted by somebody saying, "I'm going out to buy a newspaper," and cursing the war—thus dating the reverie. An idea or an image used in a later work drifts past on the stream; the figure of Shakespeare, meditating, reappears in *Orlando*. *Kew Gardens* is to Clive Bell the expression by an artist in words of the shapes and colors that Renoir and Monet rendered in paint; to Winifred Holtby it is evidence that Mrs. Woolf had discovered the cinematic technique of shifting the perspective from high to low, from huge to microscopic, "to let people, insects, aeroplanes, flowers, pass across the vision and melt away." *An Unwritten Novel* is an interesting anticipation of *Mr. Bennett and Mrs. Brown*, with the traveler in a railway carriage becoming interested in one of five people in the seat opposite, and making up a story about a dingy elderly spinster—"Miss Marsh"—out of the external details so important to an Arnold Bennett. But "Miss Marsh" is met at her destination by an obviously attentive son, and the story vanishes; "Miss Marsh" has escaped, as "Mrs. Brown" does later. One may seize every outward detail and get no closer to the life within.

Mrs. Woolf was approaching *Jacob's Room* by way of *Kew Gardens*. This new novel was to have "no scaffolding; scarcely a brick to be seen; all crepuscular, but the heart, the passion, humour, everything as bright as fire in the mist." (*Diary,* Jan. 26, 1920). She began it April 16, 1920, and completed it November 4, 1921. The technique astonished Lytton Strachey—"how you manage to leave out everything that's dreary, and yet retain enough string for your pearls I can hardly understand." (Letter of Oct. 9, 1922). He enumerates pearl after pearl: St. Paul's, the British Museum at night, the Parthenon; and finds Jacob successful, "in a most remarkable and original way. Of course I see something of Thoby in him, as I suppose you intended." (Jacob went up to Cambridge in October, 1906; Thoby Stephen died in Greece in the late autumn of 1906; Jacob's last adventure is in Greece, before he is drawn into the war and killed.) Strachey remarks, "Of course you're very romantic," and that brings a prompt reply: he puts his finger on the spot, she agrees; and where did she catch her romanticism? certainly not from her father; some of it comes from "the effort of breaking with complete representation. One flies into the air." These flights into the air were puzzling then, but they are not now, novel readers having lived through much more erratic ascents. A few of the flights in *Jacob's Room* are flops rather than flights, but others are magnificent. The cinematic technique—the camera sometimes sweeping over crowds, then focusing on an individual or a group, now giving a close-up of a little scene and again ranging the heavens—is no longer an obstacle to comprehension. But sometimes the flight in *Jacob's Room* takes off from goodness knows where and lands nowhere—or so it seems. There remain what Strachey calls the pearls, and the string, thematic or chronological, holds them together. Add to Strachey's list the scene in the boat off the Scilly Isles with the two young men; the entire Cambridge section; the British Museum Reading Room by day; sordid Soho by night. Mrs. Woolf is not trying to portray the character of Jacob in any of the long-established ways; perhaps she is only using Jacob to find an answer to her insistent question—what is the spirit we live by? The title has a meaning beyond the actual rooms where Jacob lived or worked or visited his friends. His "room" is a bench on a sunny day in Hyde Park; a seat on the upper deck of an Oxford Street bus; a pew in King's College Chapel; a box at the Covent Garden opera. It is the "outer"—"the semi-transparent envelope surrounding us from the beginning of consciousness to the end." It is also the people who touch Jacob's life, intimately or tangentially: his mother; his tutor; his college friend Timothy Durrant; Bonamy, the friend who does not care for women; the several women who love him, each after her fashion, though with only one does he seem to be in love; but he is killed too soon for us ever to know whether that was really love. It is the books he reads, and all the beauty and the ugliness that we assume he responds to in the world of Cambridge and London and Greece. For we do not enter into his mind and only guess at what goes on there. Jacob reads Plato in his London room late at night: "when at length one reads straight ahead, falling into step, marching on, becoming (so it seems) momentarily part of this rolling imperturbable energy, which has driven darkness before it since Plato walked the Acropolis, it is impossible to see the fire.... The dialogue draws to its close.... Plato's argument is stowed away in Jacob's mind, and for five minutes Jacob's mind continues, alone, into the darkness." Then he parts the curtains and looks out the window; and it may be that he thinks of the British Museum where he had been reading Marlowe that afternoon—or it may be Virginia Woolf who thinks of it as "a vast mind sheeted with stone." "Stone lies solid over the British Museum, as bone lies cool over the visions and heat of the brain. Only here the brain is Plato's brain and Shakespeare's; the brain has made pots and statues, great bulls and little jewels, and crossed the river of death this way and that incessantly, seeking some landing, now wrapping the body well for its long sleep; now laying a penny piece on the eyes; now turning the toes scrupulously to the East."

In the later novels, we know, even without explicit indication, whose consciousness among the characters we are for the moment living with. But in *Jacob's Room* we have only hints of the later distinctions—the idioms of thought and image—which create for us the unique individual.

Jacob, the little boy on the beach at Scarborough, is first called into being by his brother's shout—Ja-cob, Ja-cob! "The voice had an extraordinary sadness. Pure from all body, pure from all passion, going out into the world, solitary, unanswered, breaking against rocks—so it sounded." And at the end we hear the voice of his friend Bonamy, speaking his name in the empty room. In the time between, Jacob is perhaps most fully realized as a person in the Cambridge section. We see him late at night in a friend's room, smoking his pipe, listening to the late hour stroked by the clock, satisfied after an argument; then changing his expression slightly—"the sound of the clock conveying (it may be) a sense of old buildings and time; and himself the inheritor; and then tomorrow and friends." Turning back into the room, which was full of intimacy, still, deep, like a pool, he continues the argument, until he leaves to cross the court back to his own rooms, his footsteps ringing out, "as if the old stone chapel echoed with magisterial authority: 'The young man—the young man—back to his rooms.'" The young man among his elders is acutely conscious of youth. With three fellow undergraduates he is entertained at Sunday luncheon in the home of one of the dons. When they escape, Jacob voices their feelings in his exclamation—"O God!"—at the boredom of such a world, such an unnecessary world. Insolent and inexperienced, the author calls him, reflecting on the shock with which the world of the elderly comes upon the young of twenty, whether undergraduate or shop boy, "thrown up in such black outline upon what we are; upon the reality; the moors and Byron; the sea and the light-house." The elderly will try to prevent the young from making their own world, will sit on their heads; Wells and Shaw and the sixpenny weeklies lie on the tables of the dons. But the bored young men escape to the walk by the river and the reassurance of the trees and the gray spires and the air of May, and so to lazy reading and daydreaming in the boat moored under the trees. One must agree that Mrs. Woolf was very generous in entering so unreservedly into the pleasure of these privileged young men, when one remembers how the beadles of "Oxbridge" waved her off the grass and away from the Library and put the female in her place.

Her own pleasure in the Cambridge scene comes to us through Jacob. Included in *A Cambridge Scrapbook*—an anthology of selections about the Cambridge of the years before 1939—are three long quotations from *Jacob's Room* and

A *Room of One's Own*. Jean Lindsay, who made the collection, writes: "Perhaps it is not quite fair to quote Virginia
Woolf's descriptions of Cambridge as illustrating the reac-
tions of undergraduates, but they express feelings that have
certainly stirred in some undergraduates as they watched the
light through the windows of King's Chapel softly chalking
the stone red, yellow and purple, or saw the spring flowers
tossing in the long grass of a College wilderness. . . . Perhaps
only Virginia Woolf saw 'the sky washed into the crevices of
King's College Chapel' as being 'lighter, thinner, more sparkling than the sky elsewhere.' " [6] Jacob's own thoughts in the
Chapel are far from reverent. He reveres truth, nevertheless,
even when it comes out of very odd vessels. "If any light
burns above Cambridge," it shines from rooms where, in one,
Greek burns, in another, science; philosophy on the ground
floor. Poor old Huxtable cannot walk straight, Cowan still
chuckles at the same old stories; Sopwith has praised the sky
any night for twenty years. But what a procession of ideas
tramps through the corridors of Huxtable's brain, "orderly,
quick-stepping, and reinforced, as the march goes on, by fresh
runnels, till the whole hall, dome, or whatever one calls it,
is populous with ideas. Such a muster takes place in no
other brain." And Sopwith, entertaining undergraduates till
midnight in his room, goes on talking, "as if everything could
be talked—the soul itself slipped through the lips in thin
silver disks which dissolve in young men's minds like silver,
like moonlight." Cowan could intone without book Virgil,
Catullus, "as if language were wine on his lips . . . holding up
in his snug little mirror the image of Virgil, all rayed round
with good stories of the dons of Trinity and red beams of
port." Outside these charmed circles is old Miss Umphelby,

6 A *Cambridge Scrapbook*. Collected by Jean Lindsay (Enlarged
ed.; Cambridge: W. Heffer & Sons, 1960). Other selections are from the
writings of E. M. Forster, J. M. Keynes, Lowes Dickinson, and Sir
Leslie Stephen.

sauntering along the Backs on her way to Newnham or Girton, who can intone Virgil melodiously enough, but whose lectures are not as popular as Cowan's—for there were restrictions that kept women from telling all they knew. "So that if at night, far out at sea over the tumbling waves, one saw a haze on the waters, a city illuminated, a whiteness even in the sky, such as that now over the Hall of Trinity where they're still dining, or washing up plates, that would be the light burning there—the light of Cambridge."

Jacob is not lost in London, but rather diminished, although sharply realized at certain moments, as when he meets Florinda around the Guy Fawkes bonfire or emerges with her from his bedroom, refreshed and cheerful—for Mrs. Woolf has a quite un-Victorian detachment and candor about such matters. We know little about what he actually does in his City office. He passes easily, like the young men of his class in pre-1914 England, from the adventure of education to the adventures of sex, travel, different kinds of friendship, and love. His recorded remarks are few; such as his exclamation of disgusted boredom after the don's luncheon party, or of quiet appreciation of the scene in Hyde Park on a June afternoon: " 'Very urbane,' Jacob brought out." And to his friend Bonamy the word "urbane" on the lips of Jacob had "all the shapeliness of a character which Bonamy thought daily more sublime . . . though he was still, and perhaps would be for ever, barbaric, obscure." We know that Jacob discusses matters of import with his friends, because of little phrases like "it follows" (followed by dots), which sprinkle the page. But what were they discussing? When he is reading Marlowe in the British Museum, something of his ambition to write and his youthful self-confidence comes through: "There is Mr. Masefield, there is Mr. Bennett. Stuff them into the flame of Marlowe and burn them to cinders. . . . Don't palter with the second rate. Detest your own age. Build a better one. And to set that on foot read incredibly

H

dull essays upon Marlowe to your friends. For which purpose one must collate editions in the British Museum. One must do the thing oneself. Useless to trust to the Victorians, who disembowel, or to the living, who are mere publicists. The flesh and blood of the future depends entirely upon six young men. And as Jacob was one of them, no doubt he looked a little regal and pompous as he turned his page." He writes an essay on literary indecency, defending it, but after an evening in the sordid atmosphere of Soho he feels a strong reversion to cloistered rooms and the classics and male society—till Florinda lays a hand on his knee.

People who meet Jacob even casually are impressed by something in his air that is distinguished, though he is awkward and more often silent than not. "If he is going to get on in the world, he will have to find his tongue," remarks one hostess. How are we to know Jacob? How indeed are we to know anybody? "It seems that a profound, impartial, and absolutely just opinion of our fellow-creatures is utterly unknown. Either we are men, or we are women. Either we are cold, or we are sentimental. Either we are young, or growing old. In any case life is but a procession of shadows, and God knows why it is that we embrace them so eagerly, and see them depart with such anguish, being shadows. And why, if this and much more than this is true, why are we yet surprised in the window corner by a sudden vision that the young man in the chair is of all things in the world the most real, the most solid, the best known to us—why indeed? For the moment after we know nothing about him. Such is the manner of our seeing. Such the conditions of our love." Jacob's "room" is more vividly realized than Jacob. Presented chiefly through his surroundings and the often fleeting impressions he makes upon others, and doomed by an "inexorable force" to a brief passage through time, Jacob escapes us. We leave his empty room, where his mother, holding up a pair of his old shoes, asks, "What am I to do with these, Mr. Bonamy?"

IV

Mr. and Mrs. Dalloway were still young when they left the steamer on *The Voyage Out*, after contributing to Rachel Vinrace's development. Clarissa was about fifty when she went shopping in Bond Street, as recorded in the *Dial*, May, 1923—"Mrs. Dalloway in Bond Street." A few phrases in the later novel first shaped themselves in this little piece of London strolling. That Clarissa had continued to interest Mrs. Woolf is suggested by four brief sketches, three of which were first published in the posthumous *A Haunted House and Other Stories*.[7] Here is Mrs. Dalloway's house in Westminster, a center of social life, and Mrs. Dalloway, the charming hostess: she introduces a couple of people; tells a guest that it is too early to go; other guests have a conversation in the back garden; Richard Dalloway invites a friend to a party. When the novel began to take shape in her mind, she first thought of the title as *The Hours*—very appropriate, considering the part played by Big Ben. She recalled in her *Diary*, June 18, 1925, a night at Rodmell when she decided to give it up, "because I find Clarissa in some way tinselly. Then I invented her memories. But I think some distaste for her persisted."

There was a theory once current that *Mrs. Dalloway* was the outcome of deliberate experiment with a new method. But in her preface to the Modern Library edition (1928), she says that her idea "started as the oyster starts or the snail to secrete a house for itself. And this it did without any conscious direction." Several entries in the *Diary* record its progress. "Mrs. Dalloway has branched out into a book; and

7 "The New Dress," "Together and Apart," "The Man Who Loved His Kind," "A Summing Up." "The New Dress" was published first in *Forum*. May, 1927.

I adumbrate here a study of insanity and suicide; the world seen by the sane and the insane side by side—something like that" (Oct. 14, 1922). "I expect I could have screwed *Jacob* up tighter, if I had foreseen; but I had to make my path as I went" (Oct. 29, 1922). "I want to give life and death, sanity and insanity; I want to criticise the social system, and to show it at work, at its most intense. But here I may be posing. . . . I foresee . . . that this is going to be the devil of a struggle. The design is so queer and so masterful. I'm always having to wrench my substance to fit it" (June 19, 1923). By August 30 she has made a discovery: "how I dig out beautiful caves behind my characters: I think that gives exactly what I want; humanity, humour, depth. The idea is that the caves shall connect and each comes to daylight at the present moment"—and the present moment is one June day in London (she had read *Ulysses*). On October 15, in the thick of the mad scene in Regent's Park, she is worried about the character of Clarissa, which is perhaps too stiff, too glittering, too tinselly; "But then I can bring innumerable other characters to her support. . . . It took me a year's groping to discover what I call my tunnelling process, by which I tell the past by instalments, as I have need of it." She completed the novel in October, 1924, and in November, retyping and driving her way through the mad chapters, she wondered "whether the book would have been better without them." The opinions expressed by Leonard Woolf and by Lytton Strachey, and set down in the *Diary*, may be shared by some readers. Mr. Woolf thought it had more continuity than *Jacob's Room* but was difficult owing to the lack of visible connection between the two themes (Jan. 6, 1925). Strachey did not like it and she liked him all the better for saying so; he found a discordancy between the ornament (extremely beautiful) and what happens (rather ordinary or unimportant), caused by "some discrepancy in Clarissa herself; he thinks she is disagreeable and limited, but that I alternately

laugh at her and cover her, very remarkably, with myself"
(June 18, 1925).

Mrs. Dalloway, the best known of Mrs. Woolf's novels, is
yet seldom mentioned as their favorite by her admirers, who
prefer *To the Lighthouse* or *The Waves* or even *Between the
Acts*. It has been widely translated—into French, Danish,
Dutch, German, Finnish, Hungarian, Italian, Portuguese,
and Spanish. One interesting thing about it is amusingly
pointed up by the bald title of the German translation: *Eine
Frau von Fünfzig Jahren—Mrs. Dalloway*. Ladies of fifty, and
respectable at that, are not usually cast as heroines. But
Clarissa's husband still loves her, her old lover Peter Walsh,
returning after years of service in India, feels a renewal of
excitement when he meets her, and Clarissa herself is still
excited about living. This Frau of fifty belongs to the government class and is socially acceptable in the higher circles;
she is well known for her successful parties in her modest
house in Westminster; her husband is active in "government"; their only child, a daughter, is just ready to be introduced into society; she is giving a party the very night of the
story at which the Prime Minister is to be present, and she is
occupied during the June day with preparations abroad and
at home; a rejected lover comes unexpectedly to call upon
her, and the party brings together several other friends from
her younger days; and the party comes off successfully. What
could be very exciting about that? Though World War I has
been over for several years, the London social system still
holds together, with clear class distinctions, and the weather
is June and nice for walking. Nearly everybody walks, mostly
through the West End of London—Clarissa, Richard, Peter Walsh, Elizabeth Dalloway, Septimus Smith, the shell-
shocked soldier, and his little Italian wife, Rezia. The ground
covered includes the Green Park, Regent's Park, Russell
Square, the Strand, Piccadilly, Bond Street, Whitehall—a
very delightful tour. These seemingly unimportant happen-

ings stir memories, associations, reflections, and feelings in the minds of the different characters, so that the inner and the outer aspects of experience are interwoven. Peter, for instance, walking to Bloomsbury for dinner at his hotel, hears the bell of the ambulance that has picked Septimus up, and reflects upon the triumphs of civilization and the communal spirit of London; and he recalls exploring London with Clarissa from the top of a bus, and the talks they had had about those "unseen parts of us" that might survive; and then he thinks of other meetings with Clarissa in the old days, brief and interrupted, but now, in memory and in absence, blossoming out with understanding, "after years of lying lost." So later in the evening, at the end of the party, we can feel with Peter the mingling of terror and ecstasy at the sight of Clarissa—the extraordinary excitement.

Paths cross. Septimus and Rezia see the same airplane as Clarissa, at the same moment; stand on the curb with her to let a royal car pass; sit on a bench in Regent's Park where Peter is resting; and Septimus, driven over the edge by the ministrations of a famous psychiatrist, jumps from a window on the very night of the party, at which the psychiatrist, a guest, mentions this very sad case, and shocks Clarissa with the thought "death at my party." There are deeper connections between Clarissa and Septimus, suggested by patterns of imagery in their consciousness. The original idea, as Mrs. Woolf tells us in the preface to the Modern Library edition, was that Clarissa would kill herself; but in some odd way Septimus entered the picture and became Clarissa's double, a surrogate suicide. Mrs. Woolf was reading Dostoevsky about this time, and the Double is a very Dostoevskian conception. Septimus has slipped beneath the surface where Clarissa still keeps her footing. "She felt somehow very like him. . . . She felt glad he had done it—thrown it away." She has a brief moment of self-realization, of how her own life has been tarnished by lies, chatter, corruption, scheming.

Septimus has preserved something she has lost, and his death is a defiance of the evil represented by Sir William Bradshaw, the psychiatrist—a portrait etched with malice and hatred of those who dominate others, especially under cover of humanity. "Naked, defenceless, the exhausted, the friendless, received the impress of Sir William's will. He swooped; he devoured. He shut people up. It was this combination of decision and humanity that endeared Sir William so greatly to the relations of his victims."

Several decisions are made that day in the interrelated lives: Elizabeth Dalloway passes over one of the shadow lines between youth and maturity, for she sees—aided by a solitary London ride and walk through the anonymous crowds—what she wants to do in life; Peter Walsh, who had come home thinking he was going to marry a grass widow, abandons that idea when he sees Clarissa; and the fate of Septimus and his pathetic wife is decided. The significance of these things can be brought out only by exploring the stream of consciousness as it is influenced by the stream of events. And Mrs. Woolf's skill at this exploration is—rather suddenly, it seems, when we recall *Night and Day*—masterly. She has perfected her instrument, and it only remained to use it on material of deeper meaning.

That *Mrs. Dalloway* is a good deal less simple than it seems is evident from what the image and symbol seekers find to explicate. Critics have laid bare a structure susceptible of geometrical diagraming, and a symbolism so precisely worked out as to seem almost mechanical. Since what happens in the novel does not hold the reader in great suspense, he may well—especially on a second reading—enjoy studying the diagrams and searching for the relevant images. David Daiches diagrams the two dimensions of space and time: "We either stand still in time and are led to contemplate diverse but contemporaneous events in space, or we stand

still in space and are allowed to move up and down tem-
porally in the consciousness of one individual." Or we may
substitute *personality* for space, and work with time and
personality. In some sections time is fluid and personality
stable, in others personality is fluid and time is stable. Say
that at one point we are halted at the curb of a London street
and take a peep into the minds of a variety of unconnected
people, just happening to be at the same place at the same
time; while at another moment we move up and down, back
and forth in time within one person's memory.[8]

Or consider images. Irene Simon, "Some Aspects of Virginia Woolf's Imagery," examines in detail the imagery in
Mrs. Dalloway and *To the Lighthouse*.[9] Her interpretation
is based on what she considers Mrs. Woolf's main themes:
life and death, time and the absolute, confusion and order,
singleness and oneness (or merging). "Sometimes the meaning of the image cannot be grasped until a scene from the
past is evoked, a scene which the present emotion recalls."
Is the identification of Clarissa and Septimus arbitrary? It is
helped by the recurrence of the lines from the dirge in
Cymbeline—"Fear no more"—in Clarissa's reverie, when she
is quietly sewing at home, and in Septimus's, when, for a
moment at peace, he is watching his wife sewing. Clarissa:
"'Fear no more,' says the heart, committing its burden to
some sea, which sighs collectively for all sorrows, and renews,
begins, collects, lets fall. And the body alone listens to the
passing bee; the wave breaking; the dog barking." And Septimus: "The sound of water was in the room and through
the waves came the voices of birds singing ... and his hand
lay there on the back of the sofa, as he had seen his hand lie
when he was bathing, floating, on the top of the waves, while
far away on shore he heard dogs barking.... Fear no more,

8 David Daiches, "Virginia Woolf," in *The Novel and the Modern
World*.
9 *English Studies* (Holland), Vol. XLI, No. 3 (June, 1960).

says the heart to the body; fear no more." A link is forged between the worlds of the sane and the insane.

Some sea images are merely beautiful—not symbolic. Peter walks from Bloomsbury to Westminster on a lovely June evening to Clarissa's party, in the yellow-blue evening light that shone on the leaves in the square, and "they looked as if dipped in sea water—the foliage of a submerged city." Clarissa in her silver-green dress, escorting her Prime Minister, moves among her guests with the ease of a creature floating in its element. "But age had brushed her; even as a mermaid might behold in her glass the setting sun on some very clear evening over the waves."

If you prefer roses to waves, here too the harvest is rich. Barbara Seward, in her study *The Symbolic Rose*, notes that Virginia Woolf "used the rose throughout her novels as a minor but recurrent symbol of a highly personal fulfillment." The rose appears at intense moments when her characters realize "the ineffable meanings of their lives." These are moments of true vision, expressing her own conviction that "ecstasy, solitude, love, and death are interchangeable aspects of life, and that only by accepting the kinship between things that seem diverse can the individual attain his highest possible fulfillment. Her rose is a symbol of affirmation but her affirmation embraces both anguish and ecstasy. For in the end it makes little difference whether it is 'a rose or a ram's skull' carved over the door to Jacob's room. The universal symbols of fruition and death refer in Virginia Woolf to the same reality." At significant points in *Mrs. Dalloway* roses are associated with both Clarissa and Septimus.[10]

Perhaps the old lady who lives across the street from Mrs. Dalloway, and whom she sometimes, in idle moments, watches going about her preparations for the night, is not precisely a symbol; but she is, in an elusive way, like "Mrs. Brown" in the railway carriage, "life itself," and we see her

10 Barbara Seward, *The Symbolic Rose*, pp. 127-31.

when we look out the window upon "life in general." On the
night of the party Clarissa, disturbed by Sir William Bradshaw's mention of Septimus's suicide, and shaken by thoughts
of death and pain and their meaning, leaves the drawing
room for the little room where the Prime Minister had gone
with Lady Bruton. But the room is empty; the party's
splendor fell to the floor; it was so strange to be alone with
her finery. She parts the curtains, sees the old lady moving
about in the room opposite, looks at the "ashen pale sky raced
over quickly by tapering vast clouds." It was fascinating,
"with people still laughing and shouting in the drawing-
room, to watch that old woman, quite quietly, going to bed.
She pulled the blind now. The clock began striking. The
young man had killed himself; but she did not pity him. . . .
There! the old lady had put out her light! the whole house
was dark now with this going on, she repeated, and the words
came to her, Fear no more the heat of the sun. She must
go back to them. But what an extraordinary night!"

v

On the day *Mrs. Dalloway* was published, May 14, 1925,
Mrs. Woolf notes in her *Diary* her desire to "get on to *To
the Lighthouse*. This is going to be fairly short; to have
father's character done complete in it; and mother's; and St.
Ives; and childhood; and all the usual things I try to put in—
life, death, etc." And June 27, "The sea is to be heard all
through it."

Deserting London, Mrs. Woolf places her characters by
the sea, in a spot as remote as the San Marina of her first
novel, and so draws a magic circle around them. Is it an
island off the coast of Scotland? David Daiches, in his *Virginia Woolf*, has tried to pin down this island in the north-
west of Scotland, using clues in the text, but finds it impossible to be certain. The scene is either "a composite one (with

perhaps some suggestions from Cornwall) or largely imaginary." There is a lighthouse on a little island within sailing distance from the village and the summer home of the Ramsays. The time in the first movement of the story is a summer before the First World War. Mr. and Mrs. Ramsay, their eight children, and several guests fill the house to overflowing. Part I—"The Window"—takes up one day and ends with the quiet communion of husband and wife after the dinner which has drawn them all together into a harmony that is the triumph of Mrs. Ramsay's gift of creating an atmosphere in which barriers between people vanish. Earlier in the day Mrs. Ramsay is seated at the window entertaining her youngest son James with fairy stories; Lily Briscoe, an artist, is outside painting the window scene; Mr. Ramsay is stalking up and down upon the terrace, reciting scraps of poetry when he is blocked in his philosophical speculations; and the children and other guests drift past on their own business. James hopes for a trip to the lighthouse tomorrow, and when his father announces that the weather will be bad, James hates him and feels that it would be a pleasure to kill him with the scissors he is cutting out pictures with; for he has disturbed "the perfect simplicity and good sense of his relations with his mother." In the course of the day we dip into the reveries of most of the characters and come to distinguish one from another as readily as if they were identified by some mannerism of speech or gesture or physical peculiarity. Jane Austen, said Mrs. Woolf, "went in and out of her people's minds like the blood in their veins," and so does Mrs. Woolf, though her way of doing it is very different. They all dine, except for the smallest children, in the candlelighted room that evening, Mrs. Ramsay bringing the whole group of separate and constrained individualities together by her tact; "the whole effort of merging and flowing and creating rested on her."

They do not go to the lighthouse. Years pass. The house

remains empty except for the occasional visits of the caretaker. Things happen, parenthetically, to the human beings
who had peopled the house that summer. Mrs. Ramsay dies
suddenly one night. Her lovely daughter Prue dies in child-
birth; her son Andrew is destroyed in a moment by a shell in
the war. Ten years later some of the same guests, those of the
children who are left, and Mr. Ramsay gather again in the
house, rescued from decay by the heroic efforts of two old
cleaning women; and James at last goes to the lighthouse—
against his will, hating his father for making him go as he
had hated him before for preventing the trip. But against his
will, too, he is pleased when his father praises his skill in
steering. Lily Briscoe puts the last stroke to the painting of
the window begun ten years earlier.

Quite early in her work upon the novel Mrs. Woolf had
conceived of it in three parts—Mrs. Ramsay living, Mrs.
Ramsay dead, and the years between. And these years were
to be "this impersonal thing, which I am dared to do by my
friends, the flight of time and the consequent break of unity
in my design" (Diary, July 20, 1925). That interlude, "Time
Passes," proved to be the most difficult abstract piece of writing—"I have to give an empty house, no people's characters,
the passage of time, all eyeless and featureless with nothing
to cling to" (Diary, April 30, 1926). The two main parts, in
Winifred Holtby's phrase, "are fitted like two mirrors, the
second reflecting the first, fastened together by the hinge of
passing time." [11]

Let us watch Mrs. Ramsay at her dinner table, before the
candles are lighted, when the diners are at odds and separate
beneath the conventional mask of politeness. Mrs. Ramsay
knows when Mr. Ramsay is irritated; when Rose or Roger is
on the brink of breaking out into laughter; when young Mr.
Tansley's vanity is making him uneasy, fidgeting because he
wants somebody to give him a chance to assert himself; when

[11] Holtby, Virginia Woolf, p. 141.

Lily Briscoe, sitting opposite him, sees right through him but won't help him because he had said that women can't paint, can't write; and then Mrs. Ramsay looks at her and in effect says, I am drowning, my dear! say something nice to that young man or life will run upon the rocks!—so Lily does say something nice, feels Mrs. Ramsay's gratitude, and her spirits rise at the thought of painting tomorrow; and so it goes around the table. Mrs. Ramsay fills up the gaps, averts the collisions, exchanges glances with her husband, each knowing exactly what the other feels. Everyone is uneasy because Paul and Minta—on the verge of falling in love—have not come in from the beach, and in the midst of it all old Mr. Bankes, the poet, makes the disconcerting request for another plate of soup. Then Mrs. Ramsay asks Rose and Roger to light the candles—the eight candles down the long table with its yellow and purple dish of fruit in the middle. The faces are brought nearer by the candlelight and "composed, as they had not been in the twilight, into a party round a table, for the night was now shut off by panes of glass, which, far from giving any accurate view of the outside world, rippled it so strangely that here, inside the room, seemed to be order and dry land; there, outside, a reflection in which things wavered and vanished, waterily. Some change at once went through them all, as if this had really happened, and they were all conscious of making a party together in a hollow, on an island; had their common cause against the fluidity out there." Their faces have "the bright mask-like look of faces seen by candlelight."

Paul and Minta finally come in; they are engaged, and Mrs. Ramsay has in a way brought it about, for she likes to arrange things—a weakness, Lily thinks. The dinner takes on the quality of a festival, a celebration, crowned by the serving of the Boeuf en Daube, a delectable dish made from a recipe handed down from Mrs. Ramsay's French grandmother. Lily feels that there is something a little frightening about Mrs.

Ramsay in her triumph; as if, having brought about this engagement, she is leading her victims to the altar; and meanwhile—an ironical touch—Mrs. Ramsay is thinking of another possible marriage, between Lily and Mr. Bankes: "William must marry Lily. They have so much in common. Lily is so fond of flowers. They are both cold and aloof and rather self-sufficient. She must arrange for them to take a long walk together." Everything seems to her just right for the moment. An element of joy rises like smoke, holding them safe together; "there is a coherence in things, a stability; something, she meant, is immune from change, and shines out (she glanced at the window with its ripple of reflected lights) in the face of the flowing, the spectral, like a ruby; so that again tonight she had the feeling she had had once today, already, of peace, of rest. Of such moments, she thought, the thing is made that endures."

The conversation flows on beyond the moment, and she is again aware of hidden shoals and reefs, of the need to protect her husband's vanity; and she listens with admiration to the talk about things of which she knows little—"this admirable fabric of the masculine intelligence." Her husband is in great spirits, exchanging stories with his old friend Augustus Carmichael about someone they had both known at college. Her attention wanders and she looks at the window "in which the candle flames burnt brighter now that the panes were black, and looking at that outside, the voices came to her very strangely, as if they were voices at a service in a cathedral."

The movement into the "Time Passes" interlude is gradual. Mr. Bankes, young Andrew, Prue, Lily, who had gone out after dinner to look at the sea, come in from the terrace. "Almost too dark to see.... One can hardly tell which is the sea and which the land ... do we leave that light burning—no, not if everyone's in—put out the light in the hall." Old Mr. Carmichael, who likes to lie awake reading Virgil, keeps his candle burning longer than the rest. "So with the lamps all put out, the moon sunk, and a thin rain drumming on the roof, a downpouring of immense darkness began." The house lies in the darkness with its sleepers. And then begins the gradual subsidence into the stream of time and decay. Night follows night, season, season. Nights of destruction, of tossing seas; days of turning lights and shadows, of loveliness and stillness. "The mantle of silence ... week after week in the empty room wove into itself the falling cries of birds, ships hooting, the drone and hum of the fields, a dog's bark, a man's shout, and folded them round the house in silence." The empty house, visited by the winds and storms of many winters, stroked at regular intervals by the beams from the lighthouse, falls into decay from damp and dust, until it is touch and go whether the process will be completed and the house will pitch down into darkness. A pair of shoes, a shooting cap, some faded skirts in wardrobes—these alone keep the human shape. Memories of Mrs. Ramsay lingering about the house come to life only when the old cleaning women recall this or that trivial detail about her, and then "faint and flickering, like a yellow beam or the circle at the end of a telescope, a lady in a grey cloak, stooping over her flowers, went wandering over the bedroom wall, up the dressing-table, across the washstand, as Mrs. McNab hobbled and ambled, dusting and straightening." So the procession of nights and days and seasons passes before us; and what happens to the human beings who had filled the house and gathered around the candlelighted dinner table is lightly touched on in a parenthesis here and there, like a poetic or ironic mark of punctuation in the long record of time. Lovely summer days drift by; sunsets on the sea, fishing boats against the moon. Then the apparition of an ashen-colored ship—come, gone, leaving a purplish stain on the bland surface of the sea, as if something had boiled and bled invisibly beneath. ("Mr. Carmichael brought out a volume of poems that spring, which had an unexpected success. The war, people said, had revived their interest in poetry.")

At last one day the house, rescued, is reopened. While the boat carries Mr. Ramsay and the now almost grown-up James and Cam to the lighthouse, and that little drama of reconciliation plays itself out, Lily sets up her easel on the terrace and works upon the unfinished painting of Mrs. Ramsay and James at the window, begun ten years ago. "As she dipped into the blue paint, she dipped too into the past." Mr. Ramsay had distressed her that morning by his half-conscious demand upon her for the sympathy his wife always had ready for him. It had seemed that "his immense self-pity, his demand for sympathy, poured and spread itself in pools at her feet, and all she did, miserable sinner that she was, was to draw her skirts a little closer around her ankles, lest she should get wet." She is distressed, too, that she can feel no emotion over Mrs. Ramsay's death. The course of her reverie leads through a very subtle complex of associated ideas and recalled emotions—partly directed by the fresh impressions coming to her from the scene around her—to the final overwhelming sense of loss, and then to a release from pain. She completes the painting; and to her, the glimpse of truth has been made clear through the relation of masses, lights, and shadows. All passes; "but not words, not paint." She reflects that Mrs. Ramsay's gift had been to make of the moment something memorable; she had made life stand still for a moment and take a shape—one of "the thousand shapes of love."

VI

Had Mrs. Woolf succeeded in saying within the framework of a novel all she wished to say about life and death and time and personality? "I have an idea," she wrote when "making up" *To the Lighthouse*, "that I will invent a new name for my books to supplant 'novel.' A new ———— by Virginia Woolf. But what? Elegy?" (*Diary*, June 27, 1925.) She chose to call *Orlando*, her next book, a biography. A most unorthodox biography, it was perhaps a response to Lytton Strachey's suggestion to try something wilder and more fantastic than *Mrs. Dalloway*, in a "framework that admits of anything, like *Tristram Shandy*" (*Diary*, June 18, 1925). After completing *To the Lighthouse* she felt "the need of an escapade after these serious experimental books whose form is always so closely considered. I want to kick up my heels and be off. I want to embody all those innumerable little ideas and tiny stories which flash into my mind at all seasons. I think this will be great fun to write; and it will rest my head before starting the very serious, mystical poetical work which I want to come next" (March 14, 1927). By October the exciting device had entered her mind of a biography beginning in the year 1500 and continuing to the present day, called *Orlando:* "Vita; only with a change from one sex to another." Vita Sackville-West, writing in the *Listener* of January 27, 1955, says that the idea of *Orlando* was "inspired by her own strange conception of myself, my family, and Knole, my family home. Such things as old families and great houses held a sort of Proustian fascination for her.... They satisfied her acute sense of the continuity of history, English history in particular." [12] By October 22 she was launched: "I walk making up phrases; sit, contriving scenes; am in short in the thick of the greatest rapture known to me.... I am writing *Orlando* in a mock style very clear and plain, so that people will understand every word. But the balance between truth and fantasy must be careful. It is based on Vita, Violet Trefusis, Lord Lascelles, Knole, etc." She was writing the third chapter of *Orlando* a couple of months later (Dec. 20),

12 The MS of *Orlando* is in Vita Sackville-West's possession; in this article she quotes an unpublished passage or two. In Virginia Woolf's will it has been left to Knole. See Pippett, *The Moth and the Star*, pp. 254 ff.

and thinking over the scene where Orlando meets a girl in the Park and goes with her to a room in Gerrard Street; "they will talk. This will lead to a diversion or two about women's love. This will bring in O's night life." There was the problem of securing the effect of years passing; "the lights of the 18th century burning; and the clouds of the 19th century rising"; and the problem of keeping unity of tone. Yet, looking back to March, she found that "it is almost exactly in spirit, though not in actual facts, the book I planned as an escapade; the spirit to be satiric, the structure wild. Precisely." Precisely!

Orlando, hero-heroine, spans the centuries from Elizabeth I to Thursday, October 11, 1928—at that moment aged thirty-six and a lady. At any point in his surprising career, Orlando is no more alive than his historic house, where "the light airs which forever moved about the galleries stirred the blue and green arras, so that it looked as if the huntsmen were riding and Daphne were flying." Exploring the stream of consciousness is still a salient feature of Mrs. Woolf's technique. But in this book it is her own consciousness. It is her own mind that fascinates her; as she says of Sterne, his own mind fascinates him—"its oddities and its whims, its fancies and its sensibilities; and it is his own mind that colours the book and gives it walls and shape." But she is also fascinated by the long story of English literature; by London in its many changes through the years; by the curious likenesses and differences between men and women; and by the psychology of the artist. Orlando has hundreds of Mrs. Dalloway's moments of illumination; Jacob's room has become a mansion of a thousand chambers; and the river up which Rachel journeyed is the stream of English life and thought for three centuries and more. Orlando experiences almost everything but birth and death—unless one considers his change of sex birth or death: love, happy and defeated; desire for fame; disillusionment that turns him for a time from men to dogs and nature; ambassadorial splendors; profound meditations on his high hill where the oak tree stood about which he wrote his secular poem, *The Oak Tree*; the joy of creating material beauty all about him; the urge to seek the strange and exotic, and the yearning to come home again; pleasure in the society of wits and relief in the honest company of prostitutes; the thrill of being a man and pursuing, and of being a woman and yielding; the comfort of black silk knee breeches and—but there was no comfort for Orlando in Victorian crinolines. For it was then that she found it difficult to become one with the spirit of the age, though she did, passing Buckingham Palace one day, become blushingly aware of the masculine dress she had been amusing herself in, and fled home, to wrap herself in a damask bed quilt and sit down to a dish of muffins.

Orlando is rich in imagery that invites interpretation, if one is so minded. Say that the ice floes, with their fantastic human cargo, carried out to sea on the turbulent yellow flood that followed the Great Frost in the time of Elizabeth or James, means this or that about Elizabethan or Jacobean literature. Or explicate those enchanted frozen depths during the Great Frost, where shoals of eels lay motionless in a trance, and the old bumboat woman sat with her apples in her lap, ready to serve her customers, only a blueness about her lips hinting at the truth. All the changes that Orlando witnessed are suggested by the image: "High battlements of thought, habits that seemed durable as stone, went down like shadows at the touch of another mind, and left a naked sky and fresh stars twinkling in it."

The mock-serious preface is in tune with the fantasy: the long list of grateful acknowledgments—to Mme. Lopokova (Mrs. Maynard Keynes) for correcting her Russian; and to all the other friends—including most of Bloomsbury—who helped in various ways too numerous to mention; to her nephew Quentin Bell (an old and valued collaborator in fiction)—"but the list threatens to grow too long and is already too distinguished." And to the officials of the British Museum and the Public Record Office, and to the nameless gentleman who gratuitously corrected the punctuation, the botany, the entomology, the geography, and the chronology of previous works, and who, she hopes, will not spare his services on this occasion.

October, 1928, "the present moment" at the end of *Orlando*, was the month in which Mrs. Woolf gave the lectures at Newnham and Girton, Cambridge, on "Women and Fiction," which she altered and expanded into *A Room of One's Own*, published October, 1929. The completion of *Orlando* had left her with a desire to write something about the women's movement, "in the same vein." The new book is not in the same vein, though it has its lighthearted moments and its touches of fantasy, but in theme there is a close relationship; common to both is speculation about sex, time, the position of women, the androgynous artist, literature and life. E. M. Forster, though not sympathetic with Virginia Woolf's feminism, yet allowed himself a charming flight of fancy when he gave the Rede Lecture after her death. Speaking in the Senate House at Cambridge, May 29, 1941, he wished that he could transmit some of the honor he was receiving to Virginia Woolf, who loved Cambridge, but who would have received such an honor a little mockingly, being somewhat "astringent" over the academic position of women. "Indeed, I cherish a private fancy that she once took her degree here. She, who could disguise herself as a member of the suite of the Sultan of Zanzibar, or black her face to go aboard a Dreadnought as an Ethiopian—she could surely have hoaxed our innocent praelectors, and, kneeling in this very spot, have presented to the Vice-Chancellor the exquisite but dubious head of Orlando." [13]

13 See Adrian Stephen, *The Dreadnought Hoax* (Hogarth Press, 1936).

VII

Orlando, in Mrs. Woolf's own estimation, was "a very quick brilliant book," but she had not tried to explore. And must she always explore? Yes, she thought so, because she did not have the usual reaction. But *Orlando* had taught her how to write a direct sentence, had taught her continuity and narrative, and "how to keep the realities at bay. But I purposely avoided of course any other difficulty. I never got down to my depths and made shapes square up, as I did in the *Lighthouse*" (Nov. 7, 1928). Hovering at the back of her mind for some time had been a book she thought of as *The Moths*—"an abstract mystical eyeless book: a play-poem ... if I write *The Moths* I must come to terms with these mystical feelings." For nearly two years we can follow in the *Diary* the sea change of *The Moths* into *The Waves.*[14] The *inner* and the *outer* problem bothered her, as it always did: how to select; how to get from lunch to dinner. Poets simplified by leaving practically everything out, but she wished to put everything in and yet to "saturate." A general idea takes shape: childhood, but not her own childhood; the sense of children; unreality; things oddly proportioned; "the unreal world must be all around this—the phantom waves. The Moth must come in; the beautiful single moth." Abandoning the moths, she begins to cope with the problem: who thinks it? "Am I outside the thinker? One wants some device that is not a trick." The waves are giving her as much trouble as the moths did; she is seeking for a station "whence I can set my people against time and the sea." That problem she solved by the device of the interludes: "very difficult, yet I think essential; so as to bridge and also to give a background —the sea; insensate nature." Finally she could write that the book was "resolving itself ... into a series of dramatic solil-

14 *Diary,* Aug. 12, Nov. 7 and 28, 1928; June 23, Sept. 25, Nov. 2, 1929; Jan. 26, Aug. 20, Dec. 30, 1930.

oquies," to be kept "running homogeneously in and out in
the rhythm of the waves." The end of the year (1930) found
her feeling that she had perhaps achieved "a saturated un-
chopped completeness; changes of scene, of mind, of person,
done without spilling a drop."

February 7, 1931, Mrs. Woolf recorded in her *Diary* the
end of *The Waves*, and sat "in a state of glory, and calm,
and some tears, thinking of Thoby and if I could write Julian
Thoby Stephen 1881-1906 on the first page. I suppose not. . . .
Whether good or bad, it's done. . . . I have netted that fin in
the waste of water which appeared to me over the marshes
out of my window at Rodmell when I was coming to an end
of *To the Lighthouse*."

If *Orlando* is a biography, then *The Waves* is a group
biography; and if Orlando could be by turns man and
woman, then the Six in *The Waves* could be one many-sided
personality. Were *The Waves* not classified as a novel, the
unprepared reader would be less likely to be puzzled by an
unfamiliar technique. Suppose it were entitled a Meditation
—on the nature of personality and life. But it has characters,
like a novel, and they have interrelationships. They pass their
lives in recognizable surroundings which influence their development. They grow and change, and when old they still
have within them the children they once were. They have
made choices and acted upon them, and other things have
happened to them, which they could not anticipate or avert.
There are sequences and consequences. There is no plot but
there is a pattern, one of the oldest—of growth, expectation,
fulfillment and frustration, decline. The stylized monologues
impose upon them what seems to be an almost unbroken
inner life that few of us could sustain, our own inner life
being by contrast interrupted and fragmentary. The External
is reduced to a bare minimum, filtered through the percep-
tions of each of the Six; but even at that there is a good deal
of it. First, of course, the interludes: the sea breaking on the

beach, the garden, and the birds, in the successive phases of dawn, early morning, morning, high noon, afternoon, sunset, twilight. Beautiful as it is, it teases us with a crossword puzzle of symbolism, when we try to match the imagery with the stages in the development of the characters. Perhaps Mrs. Woolf does here what a friend once warned her against, "When V. lets her style get on top of her, one thinks only of that" (*Diary*, Dec. 22, 1927). Through the monologues we become aware of the rooms in the house by the sea where the Six as children spent a summer; the garden and the woods where they played; the chapel and the schoolrooms where the boys were educated; the dormitories and halls of the dreary girls' school; the firelit rooms, the boats on the river, the old buildings of Cambridge; the country vicarage where Susan grew up and the farmhouse where she spent her married life; the orderly office where Louis built his success in the City, and the attic room where he escaped from the pressure of his facts and figures; the eating house in the City where he propped Lucretius against the bottle of Worcester sauce and tried to create some order in the chaotic scene around him; the ballrooms where Jinny danced, and Rhoda suffered her agonies of shyness; the restaurant where the Six met to say farewell to Perceval; Hampton Court where they had a reunion years after his death; crowded Oxford Street where Rhoda, lost in her own imaginings, bought the violets which she threw into the river at Greenwich as a tribute to Perceval; the Tube under Piccadilly Circus where Jinny, descending the escalator, experienced a brief moment of panic at the thought of old age approaching; the bookstalls on Shaftesbury Avenue where the scholar Neville paused to leaf through a volume of Shakespeare; and the restaurant where Bernard, an old man, sat summing up his life and the lives of his friends. We perceive this external world as through a clear glass, bathed in the translucent atmosphere of each consciousness, with-

out the sharp immediacy of similar scenes in the earlier
novels or in the later *Years*.

Once, as the *Diary* records (March 28, 1929), Mrs. Woolf
met her sister Vanessa in Tottenham Court Road, a bustling
Bloomsbury thoroughfare, "both of us sunk fathoms deep in
that wash of reflection in which we both swim about." All the
Six swim about in a wash of reflection, often in surroundings
as little hospitable one would think to the inner life as Tottenham Court Road, or that other Bloomsbury thoroughfare,
Southampton Row, down which Mrs. Woolf walked when
she had finished *The Waves*, thinking, "I have given you a
new book," for to the London street haunter that she was,
these busy streets were favorable to the creative impulse
(April 28, 1930).

Consider the Six as aspects of a multiple personality: Jinny,
Susan, and Rhoda; Bernard, Neville, and Louis. Jinny lives
in the body, with the body's imagination; she is at home in
the ballroom, treading naturally on thick carpets, sliding
easily over smooth polished floors, responding to radiance like
a fern unfurling its curled leaves, riding like a gull on the
wave, "dealing her looks adroitly here and there," with no
time to sort out all the impressions she has gathered. But as
she grows older she becomes more curious about the people
she sees in the crowded rooms: "The door goes on opening.
The room fills and fills with knowledge, anguish, many kinds
of ambition, much indifference, some despair. . . . The common fund of experience is very deep. . . . In one way or another we make this day, this Friday, some by going to the
Law Courts; others to the City; others to the nursery; others
by marching and forming fours. . . . The activity is endless.
And tomorrow it begins again. . . . Some will never come into
this room again. One may die tonight. Another will beget a
child. From us every sort of building, policy, venture, picture, poem, child, factory, will spring. Life comes; life goes;

we make life." Active herself, it is human activity that excites her occasional wonder.

Rhoda, who appears to move in the same social circles as Jinny, is alien and lost in the crowd. When a door opens, "the tiger leaps"—an image for her constant fear of the person, the experience, coming to her. She escapes; imagery of marble columns and pools on the other side of the world suggests her dream life; she is mistress of nothing but her dreams, as, when a child, she rocked her ships of rose petals in a basin of water and was mistress of her fleet. She is always seeking something she can touch, and "so draw myself across the enormous gulf into my body safely," else "I shall be blown down the eternal corridors for ever." She wonders about the knowledge Jinny has when she dances, and about the assurance Susan has, when, stooping quietly beneath the lamplight, she draws the white cotton through the eye of the needle. "They say, Yes; they say, No ... But I doubt; I tremble; I see the wild thorntree shake its shadow in the desert."

Susan knows exactly what she is and what she wants. She is rooted, not blown about. She is homesick in her girls' school and later among the snows and pines of Switzerland for the country vicarage, and she is happy, after her marriage, on the farm. She likes the stare of shepherds and of gypsy women beside a cart in the ditch, and before her marriage, she knows that her lover will come, and "to his one word I shall answer my one word. What has formed in me I shall give him. I shall have children; I shall have maids in aprons; men with pitchforks; a kitchen where they bring the ailing lambs to warm in baskets, where the hams hang and the onions glisten. I shall be like my mother, silent in a blue apron, locking up the cupboards." Yet Susan is not placid. Her emotions are simple but violent; she can hate as well as love, as, when a child, she hated Jinny whom she saw kissing Louis.

Louis is the youngest and weakest among the children; the

one left behind when the others troop off to breakfast; the one who has a curious sense of identity with those roots in the garden that go into the depths of the earth; down there, his eyes are the lidless eyes of a stone figure in a desert by the Nile. (It is scarcely necessary to say that no child could have put these strange intuitions into words.) Later it is the dark backward of time that fascinates his imagination: the history and the traditions of the human race. It is Louis among the boys at school who is aware that the stone flags in the chapel are worn by the feet of six hundred years, and who is grateful for the safeguards of tradition, because he has wild impulses—hears the sullen thud of the waves and the "chained beast" stamping on the beach. (That, at least, is one's guess at the meaning of the stamping beast.) Louis in maturity is of those who through the centuries have been the seekers and the builders of civilization; as he grows older, his sense of the continuity of human experience and of himself as part of it grows stronger; he watches "the eternal procession of women going with their attaché cases down the Strand as they went once with pitchers to the Nile." Louis and Rhoda both feel their separateness. They become lovers for a while. Bernard thinks of them as the "authentics," who exist most completely in solitude.

Louis, the best scholar of the three, does not go on to the university, being destined to retrieve in the City the failure of his father. But Bernard, both at the university and in later years, often thinks what a malevolent but searching light Louis would have thrown upon the university, and upon his own poses as a Byronic or a Tolstoyan young man. He often feels Louis's eye upon them all, "adding us up like insignificant items in some grand total.... And one day, taking a fine pen and dipping it in red ink, the addition will be complete; our total will be known; but it will not be enough." Bernard, the phrasemaker, curious about other people, always making up stories about them, needs an audience—himself, if no other is present. He is plagued, or blest, with that double consciousness of the artist, who both sees and feels and thinks and at the same time watches himself seeing and feeling and thinking; who in the very act of taking part watches himself taking part.

Neville, unlike Louis who seeks to reduce chaos to order, sees an order already existing in the world—to be discovered, not imposed. He is a precise scholar. At Cambridge he is in love with life, and with the beauty of young men especially; and he is close to Bernard at this stage, both of them seeking an identity—who among these selves am I? They try to read each other. Neville sees through Bernard's poses and Bernard is aware of the rent in his defenses made by Neville's "astonishing fine rapier." Neville will always slip into cushioned firelit rooms, with many books and one friend. He sees himself becoming a don and going with schoolmasters to Greece and lecturing on the ruins of the Parthenon; and with a flash of repugnance—or of insight—"it would be better," he thinks, "to breed horses and live in one of those red villas than to run in and out of the skulls of Sophocles and Euripides like a maggot." (He remains a scholar, but does not—though his story is a little vague here—become a don.)

All these Six, different yet complementary, look to their friend Perceval, feel his fascination, and love him in their individual ways. What he is comes to us only through them. He dies young, joining Rachel and Jacob in the company of those whose promise is unfulfilled and who leave behind them the question—what did the world lose when they died? Perceval had grace of body, the courage that goes with it, unself-consciousness; he possessed the irresistible attraction that one who seems at ease with life has for those who are plagued by doubt and inner conflict.

The moment in *The Waves* when Inner and Outer fuse, creating harmony and radiance, rounding the globe, comes with the farewell dinner to Perceval on the eve of his de-

parture for India. They have all gone different ways after
their shared school and university years, but they are still
only on the threshold of life. When they meet and wait for
Perceval, and after he comes, fragments of their childhood
experiences keep slipping into their reveries, almost as if it
were a group mind remembering. The monologues are here
close to dialogue—yet not spoken. "From these close-furled
balls of string we draw now every filament (said Louis) remembering, when we meet." They have come together to
make one thing—not enduring, for what endures?—but seen
by many eyes simultaneously. Yet each of the Six asserts himself; their self-realization is at its youthful peak. The roar
of London around them isolates them—as Louis perceives:
"Motor-cars, vans, omnibuses pass and repass continuously.
All are merged in one turning wheel of single sound. All
separate sounds—wheels, bells, the cries of drunkards, of
merry-makers—are churned into one sound, steel blue, circu-
lar. Then a siren hoots. At that shores slip away, chimneys
flatten themselves, the ship makes for the open sea."

"But India lies outside," thinks Neville. And Bernard imagines Perceval's life in India. The others see different visions,
but their thoughts are focused on Perceval, and on their own
promise as well. They experience the youthful sense of infinite time and open choice before them. It is Susan who
perceives that something irrevocable has happened; the little
heaps of sugar, the peelings of fruit, the plush rims of the
looking-glasses in the restaurant, look strange, as if she had
not seen them before; everything is fixed—"a circle has been
cast on the waters; a chain is imposed. We shall never flow
freely again." Let us hold this moment, thinks Jinny, "love,
hatred, by whatever name we call it, this globe whose walls
are made of Perceval, of youth and beauty, and something so
deep sunk within us that we shall perhaps never make this
moment out of one man again." Bernard sees them as creators, who have made "something that will join the innumer-

able congregations of past time. We too, as we put on our
hats and push open the door, stride not into chaos, but into
a world that our own force can subjugate and make part of
the illumined and everlasting road."

Perceval is thrown from his horse in India and killed.

What is it like, when someone loved is suddenly gone?
Each of the friends experiences this loss differently and is
never quite the same again. Bernard hears of Perceval's death
on the same day that his son is born. "Such is the complexity
of things that as I descend the staircase I do not know which
is sorrow, which is joy. . . . I need silence, and to be alone
and to go out, and to save one hour to consider what has
happened to my world, what death has done to my world."
So he goes out into the streets and looks at the details of a
world Perceval no longer sees. He feels the rhythm, the
throb, but for the moment he is outside the machine of
living. He thinks of what the world has lost in Perceval, who
was "borne on by a natural sense of the fitting, was indeed
a great master of the art of living so that he seems to have
lived long, and to have spread calm around him, indifference
one might almost say, certainly to his own advancement, save
that he also had great compassion." He goes into the National Gallery, seeking some answer from the paintings, but
"the perpetual solicitation of the eye" weighs upon him.
"Arrows of sensation strike from my spine, but without
order." Something lies just beyond his grasp; perhaps in some
moment of revelation after a long lifetime he may lay hands
upon it. "Ideas break a thousand times for once that they
globe themselves entire." Although bodies soon look ordinary
again, what is behind them differs—the perspective. Bernard
begins to want life around him again, and wishes to remember Perceval with someone Perceval was at ease with and
liked "(not Susan whom he loved, but Jinny rather)."

Rhoda, after hearing that Perceval has been killed, goes to
a concert, and, more successful than Bernard, finds consola-

tion in a perception of order beneath all the sensations: "There is a square; there is an oblong. The players take the square and place it upon the oblong. They place it very accurately.... Very little is left outside; the structure is now visible." But this perception of meaning will never, for Rhoda, be enough to release her from her dream of escape.

The reunion with Perceval at the dinner marks the high tide, the hot sunshine, of the progress through the day, through life. His death forces reflection, readjustment, re-assessment. To cover the declining day, two sections follow, preceding the Hampton Court reunion and the final sum-ming-up by Bernard. The essential personality of each be-comes more strongly marked as the choices before them narrow. Here is Louis: "My shoulder is to the wheel; I roll the dark before me, spreading commerce where there was chaos in the far parts of the world.... If I press on, I shall inherit a chair and a rug; a place in Surrey with glasshouses, and some rare conifer, melon or flowering tree which other merchants will envy. Yet I still keep my attic room.... There I watch the rain glisten on the tiles till they shine like a policeman's waterproof; there I see the broken windows in poor people's houses; the lean cats; some slattern squinting in a cracked looking-glass as she arranges her face for the street corner; there Rhoda sometimes comes. For we are lovers." Susan is completely absorbed in her children and her household: "Whether it is summer, whether it is winter, I no longer know by the moor grass, and the heath flower; only by the steam on the window-pane, or the frost on the win-dow-pane." There will be more children, "more baskets in the kitchen and hams ripening; and onions glistening; and more beds of lettuce and potatoes." But she sometimes wishes the weight of the sleeping house would lift from her shoul-ders, sometimes hears broken voices and laughter, and Jinny's voice as the door opens, calling "Come!" Neville lives over some of the past as he sits waiting, in front of the fire, for the one friend he must have—in spite of the meetings, the partings, that finally destroy us. There must be someone so in tune with oneself that one can point at something for the other to look at and share without talking: "to follow the dark paths of the mind and enter the past, to visit books, to brush aside their branches and break off some fruit." With all his seeking after perfection, he is not disinterested; there is always the color of some personal emotion staining the page; it is someone's voice speaking the poem—Perceval's or another's. "There is no end to the folly of the human heart—seek another, find another, you." Bernard is not of those who find satisfaction in one person; the private room bores him: "My being only glitters when all its facets are exposed to many people." He knows at the onset of middle age that he has outlived many desires, but not the desire for the ultimate answers. "Let a man get up and say, 'Behold, this is the truth,' and instantly I perceive a sandy cat filching a piece of fish in the background. Look, you have forgotten the cat, I say."

A dinner at Hampton Court brings the six middle-aged men and women together again, to remember Perceval, to wonder what each has made of life. Each is measured against the others, each wishes to impress one of the others. They all share the realization that choice is no longer possible. "Before, when we met in a restaurant with Perceval, all simmered and shook; we could have been anything. We have chosen now, or sometimes it seems the choice was made for us—a pair of tongs pinched us between the shoulders." Susan compares herself with Neville; her body had been used daily, like a tool by a good workman, all over; "seen through your pale and yielding flesh, even apples and bunches of fruit must have a filmed look, as if they stood under glass." Bernard, knowing that he, with sons and daughters, is wedged into his place in the puzzle, yet cherishes the illusion that it is only his body that is fixed; his mind is more capable than when he was young of disinterested thought: "I throw my mind out in the air as a man throws seeds in great fan-lights, falling through the purple sunset." The dinner is steeped in the atmosphere of subconscious thought, never rising to the surface to become close to spoken dialogue as it did during the earlier dinner.

After they have dined well—for they do dine—"the sharp tooth of egotism" is blunted, anxiety for the moment is at rest, life is stayed here and now, and in the silence they seem to pass beyond life. But they are soon back on shore. They go out into the darkening gardens, where lovers in the shadow of the trees are scarcely to be distinguished from the ghosts of the past—King William on his horse, court ladies sweeping the turf with their silks and satins. A disembodied mood is upon them. They pair off, Rhoda and Louis, Bernard and Susan, Neville and Jinny, and disappear along the great avenues, among the trees, in the twilight and then the moonlight. It is all a dissolving dream. And it comes with something of a shock when we join Bernard and Susan, pacing the terrace by the river, and come back to life in general—watching the lights coming on in the bedrooms of small shopkeepers on the other side of the river, and imagining with Bernard the stories of the lives of all these people, who are going to sleep, thinking perhaps of their Sunday dinner (the rabbit in its hutch in the garden), or of the chance of winning the football competition. We are back to the knock, knock of one event following another, of the must of life—must go, must catch the train, must walk to the station; and we leave Bernard clasping the return half of his ticket to Waterloo—that, at least, life had taught him to hold on to.

To compare the two dinners as "moments," this seems to be a moment *manqué*. And this impression is strengthened by Bernard's recollection of it years later. He sees them all under the seduction of the wine, ceasing to measure themselves against each other, feeling around them "the huge blackness of what is outside us, of what we are not. The wind, the rush of wheels became the roar of time.... We were extinguished for a moment, went out like sparks in burnt paper and the blackness roared. Past time, past history we went." Then they become again six people at a table and rise and walk together down the avenue. Bernard sees them, against the gateway, against some cedar tree, burning there triumphant in their own identity. Then as a wave breaks, they burst asunder, surrender, draw apart, "consumed in the darkness of the trees." This is not the perfect globe. The globe of Bernard's imagining has walls of thinnest air, and, pressed, will burst.

In the final section Bernard, a rather heavy elderly man, gray at the temples, sits in a restaurant with a chance companion, for, like the Ancient Mariner, he must have an audience for his tale. "In the beginning, there was the nursery, windows opening on a garden, and beyond that the sea...." We already know the story, from six different viewpoints. Now we have it subtly modified from the one viewpoint, with the different lights and shadows and meanings that advancing years and altered perspectives have brought to the storyteller. "On the outskirts of every agony sits some observant fellow who points." Bernard is not that observant fellow, but he is one who looks where the finger points—"beyond and outside our own predicament; to that which is symbolic, and thus perhaps permanent, if there is any permanence in our sleeping, eating, breathing, so animal, so spiritual and tumultuous lives." We learn to order life, to fill up the little compartments of our engagement book, but always deep below this orderly progress, even when we arrive punctually at the appointed time, there is "a rushing stream of broken dreams, nursery rhymes, street cries, half-finished sentences and sights... that rise and sink even as we hand a lady down to dinner." The pageant of existence has never

K

ceased to fascinate Bernard; he seems to himself to have
lived many lives: "I do not altogether know who I am—
Jinny, Susan, Neville. . . . I do not always know if I am man
or woman . . . so strange is the contact of one with another."
There are moments of ebb tide, when no fin "breaks the
waste of this immeasurable sea"; moments when everything
is drained of color, of life, when the earth dies, withers.
"How then does light return to the world after the eclipse of
the sun? Miraculously. . . . The earth absorbs color like a
sponge drinking water." [15] The chance companion leaves,
and the elderly Bernard must take himself off and catch
some last train. There is the usual street, there is a stir of
dawn. "Dawn is some sort of whitening of the sky; some sort
of renewal. . . . The stars draw back and are extinguished. The
bars deepen themselves between the waves." And in the
elderly man, too, the wave rises, a new desire, a new de-
termination to meet the advancing enemy. And who could
that be now, but Death?

VIII

The Waves had been written at high pressure. The need to
relax, "to fling off on some swifter, slighter adventure," produced another "biography," that of Elizabeth Barrett Brown-
ing's spaniel Flush (1933). *The Common Reader, Second
Series,* was published in 1932; and it is not merely fanciful
to think of *Flush* as belonging with the Lives of the Obscure,
his story giving his biographer the pleasure of writing about
the Brownings from an unexpected angle. In September,
1934, Roger Fry died, and Mrs. Woolf was persuaded to
write his biography—the third of her books so entitled, but
the first that had to conform to the sober requirements of
accepted biographical literature. Years before his death, after
a discussion on the methods of the arts—discussions that

15 An eclipse of the sun is described in the *Diary*, June 30, 1927.

illuminated the long and happy friendship between Mrs. Woolf and Roger Fry—he suggested that she put into practice her theories of the biographer's craft in a portrait of himself.[16] Bernard, in *The Waves*, looking back upon his own life, makes fun of biographers: "Once I had a biographer, dead long since, but if he still followed my footsteps with his old flattering intensity he would here say, 'About this time Bernard married and bought a house.... His friends observed in him a growing tendency to domesticity.... The birth of children made it highly desirable that he should augment his income.' That is the biographic style, and it does to tack together torn bits of stuff, stuff with raw edges." He admits that one cannot despise these phrases, "laid like Roman roads across the tumult of our lives." So now Mrs. Woolf was faced with the problem of laying Roman roads across the tumult of Roger Fry's life. When it was completed, she wondered about the curious relation she now had with Roger, to whom she had given a kind of shape after his death. "Was he like that? I feel very much in his presence at the moment; as if I were intimately connected with him: as if we together had given birth to this vision of him: a child born of us. Yet he had no power to alter it. And yet for some years it will represent him" (*Diary*, July 25, 1940). After reading a favorable review in *The Times*, she felt rather proud of having done a solid work, given her friends what they wanted.

Before the book was completed in 1940, both *The Years* and *Three Guineas* were published, and the last of her novels, *Between the Acts*, began to occupy her mind. "Will another novel ever swim up? If so, how? The only hint I have towards it is that it's to be dialogue and poetry; and prose; all quite distinct" (*Diary*, Aug. 6, 1937). Her *Diary*, up to the very last entries, is a record of intellectual activity that is amazing, especially when one thinks of the increasing pres-

16 Margery Fry, Foreword, *Roger Fry*.

sure during those years of alarming political events, and the threats and reality of war. No wonder that the pendulum swings toward the External in *The Years*. First called *The Pargiters*, which suggests a family novel, it was planned to take in everything—"sex, education, life, etc.: and come with the most powerful and agile leaps, like a chamois, across precipices from 1880 to here and now" (Nov. 2, 1932). She found herself delighting in facts for a change, and finding more gold than she had thought in Externality, and more facts to be released than she had thought she had in her. But to give the whole of society, the vision as well as the facts, meant that somehow *The Waves* would have to be going on simultaneously with *Night and Day*. She had tried the "representational form" in the early novel; now she could take liberties with it that she had not dared to do then. She saw the time sequence as curiously uneven—"a series of great balloons, linked by straight narrow passages of narrative." She was still experimenting; breaking in *Here and Now* (another title for the book) the mold of *The Waves* (*Diary*, July 27, 1934).

The Years achieved, relatively speaking, a popular success in both England and the United States. Compare the figures for the first edition of *The Waves* with those for *The Years*: *The Waves*, English, 7,113, American, 10,000; [17] *The Years*, English, 18,147, American, with reimpressions, between April and October, 37,900. Of course Mrs. Woolf's reputation had been growing since *Mrs. Dalloway*—with a first English edition of 2,000 copies and an American of 2,100. But the form of *The Years* is the familiar one of the family novel, popular even when it runs on into volumes and generations. *The Years*, by contrast with Galsworthy's *Forsyte Saga* and

17 In the first year of publication, *The Waves* sold 12,000 copies in England and 12,000 in America. Leonard Woolf, *TLS*, Aug. 15, 1958. The figures for new editions and impressions of Mrs. Woolf's works are given in *A Bibliography of Virginia Woolf*.

Mann's *Buddenbrooks*, is neither dense in texture nor architecturally imposing; it is rather sketchy in fact. The leaps of the chamois over the gulf of years leave too much at times to the imagination, just as some other family chronicles leave too little. The structure suggests the Proustian method: brilliantly detailed panels devoted to a single social evening, revealing by comparison with earlier equally detailed panels all the changes that have taken place during the years between. This method may leave the reader occasionally unconvinced, but the year-by-year chronicle may leave him convinced but bored. If the creator of a character has held him in imagination for a long time, and has worked out stages in his life that are not used at all in the novel or the play—as Ibsen and Turgenev did—there will be no inconsistencies. And one feels that Mrs. Woolf knows in that way her Eleanor Pargiter, her Martin, and other members of the family.

The Pargiters are with us for about half a century, from 1880. The stretch from 1907 to 1914 is almost unbroken, with sections for 1907, 1908, 1910 (King Edward died that year), 1911, 1913, 1914 (the war began). Fifty years is long enough to cover three generations—the first, middle-aged at the beginning, passes out of the picture; the second grows up from childhood and youth to middle and old age; and the third is launched on its career as the scene closes. There are two brothers and their families to begin with: Colonel Abel Pargiter, a retired officer, his wife and seven children; and Sir Digby Pargiter, in some government position, his wife and two young daughters—with older boys offstage. (In these English families of the old Establishment, several young boys are usually at Eton or Harrow, conveniently out of the way.) There are two or three outlying cousins in the second generation; one very important one, the daughter of an Oxford professor, and later the wife of Lord Lasswade, a rather dim figure on the circumference, with an old estate in

Yorkshire. Of the Colonel's children, one son and two daughters marry. The oldest daughter, Eleanor, is the one who stays at home and holds the fort, caring for her father after her mother dies, and keeping in touch with the other members of the family, quite in the Victorian tradition, and practicing charity—an activity regarded indulgently so long as it does not interfere with family duties. Her youngest sister Rose has a different sort of spinster career in the Suffrage Movement—the militant branch; she carries on where Mary Datchet in *Night and Day* left off. Two other sisters marry conventionally and offstage. The son who marries is a member of the Bar, acquiring a nice old home in Dorsetshire with his marriage; his daughter Peggy becomes a doctor—a sign of changed times for women. His son goes out to Africa, on some farming enterprise; we see him briefly as a youth, and then much later when he returns to England, and is bewildered by the changes that have taken place.

The two daughters of Sir Digby lose their father and mother in a manner not explained—their deaths occur during one of the chamois leaps; and lose the family fortune, too. The girls are really poor, and have to make out in rather unsavory quarters of the city, introducing interesting London scenes outside of the West End, Chelsea, Highgate, and the City. Maggie, a sensible likeable girl, marries a Frenchman, of a wine-importing firm, and through him we come to know the Polish Nicholas, one of the odd men indifferent to women. He has a happy friendship, however, with Maggie's sister Sally, an eccentric girl with a gift for mimicry and often embarrassing flights of fancy. She is an important character in the novel. Through her comes the impression of a sort of dry rot in this civilization that has survived the 1914 war, but is coming apart at the seams in many ways. The two unmarried sons in the Colonel's family contribute their talents to the Army and the University, but Martin leaves the Army, to handle investments in the City and to regret that his interest in architecture had not been encouraged. This disappointment comes out in a nice scene where he contemplates St. Paul's Cathedral. His brother, the handsome Edward, is an Oxford don, a translator of Greek tragedies, and a popular conductor of educational tours to Greece. In the "Here and Now" end of the book, there is a family reunion in the furnished flat in Holborn which Delia Pargiter—who had married in Ireland—had kept for London visits. Eleanor, about seventy by this time, is the main observer, but not the only one through whom we learn what life has done to the Pargiters and their friends. Here again is a group scene. Mrs. Woolf has always handled such scenes effectively. The hotel in *The Voyage Out* lingers in the memory as very much alive with the gatherings on different occasions of the guests and their witty and revealing conversations. Such scenes furnish entertaining episodes in *Night and Day* and *Jacob's Room*, and become climaxes in Clarissa's party, Mrs. Ramsay's dinner, and the reunions in *The Waves*.

The last chapters of *The Years*, wrote Mrs. Woolf in the *Diary* (May 22, 1934), "must be so rich, so resuming, so weaving together that I can only go on by letting my mind brood every morning on the whole book. . . . What I want is to enrich and stabilise. This last chapter must equal in length and volume the first book: and must in fact give the other side, the submerged side of that." Conversations during the evening bring the submerged to the surface; groups form and separate and re-form; couples stand apart in a corner and exchange memories and comment on each other and on life; individuals, feeling for the moment out of it, withdraw and look out a window and are lost in their reveries. Eleanor, listening to the broken dialogues, picking up hints of what has happened to people of whom she knows a good deal but whose secret escapes her, and exasperated by the fragmentary nature of her knowledge even of those she knows best, thinks that there must be another life—and not just in dreams, but there, in that room, with living people. "She felt as if she were standing on the edge of a precipice with her hair blown back; she was about to grasp something that just evaded her. . . . We know nothing, even about ourselves. We're only just beginning, she thought, to understand, here and there. She hollowed her hands in her lap," with the gesture of shaping the globe. Wishing to share her thoughts with her brother Edward, but failing to attract his attention, "It's useless, she thought, opening her hands. It must drop. It must fall. And then? she thought. For her too there would be the endless night; the endless dark. She looked ahead of her as though she saw opening in front of her a very long dark tunnel. But, thinking of the dark, something baffled her; in fact it was growing light."

Before the cheerful bustle of the breaking up of the party, there is an odd and rather ambiguous episode. The two children of the caretaker are brought up from the basement, shy and awkward, to be given slices of cake. They munch the cake, stare solemnly at the grown-ups, make no response to the friendly questions. " 'The younger generation,' said Peggy, 'don't mean to speak.' " After a little prodding, they sing a song, of which not a word is recognizable—the voices harsh, the accent hideous. "There was something horrible in the noise they made. It was so shrill, so discordant, and so meaningless." And yet, as they stood there, they had looked so dignified, Eleanor thought, and did not know what to make of it. Nor do we—except as the younger generation's knock on the door is always disturbing to the older generation; and the future was beginning to look very grim in 1937. The novel does not end on that note, however, but with a view from the window of the summer dawn over the city: "The sky was a faint blue; the roofs were tinged purple against the blue; the chimneys were a pure brick red. An air of ethereal calm and simplicity lay over everything." And at the very end, "the sun had risen." (But then one remembers that it rises as the curtain falls on *Ghosts*.)

This "Present Day" section of *The Years* reads a little like "the death song of the middle classes," a phrase quoted in the *Diary* from a review in the *TLS*: "The *TLS* spoke as if it were merely the death song of the middle classes—a series of exquisite impressions" (March 14, 1937). Among the exquisite impressions that might come under this particular heading is the closing of the house on Abercorn Terrace, and the departure, on an appropriately snowy January day in 1913, of Crosby, for forty years the housekeeper and devoted family servant of the Pargiters. The house, stripped of all its furnishings, presents bleak stained and cracked walls to the young man from the House Agents who has been sent to look it over as a selling proposition. Eleanor and Crosby follow him around, resenting his derogatory comments on the sanitary arrangements of these old Victorian houses. A four-wheeler is waiting to transport Crosby and the smelly old dog Rover to her new home with a niece in Richmond. Eleanor is impatient to get it all over with, but Crosby, whose entire life since her parlormaid days has been passed in this house, wants to linger and remember. For her it is the end of everything. "She had known every cupboard, flagstone, chair and table in that large rambling house, not from five or six feet of distance as they had known it; but from her knees, as she scrubbed and polished; she had known every groove, stain, fork, knife, napkin and cupboard. They and their doings had made her entire world." Eleanor suddenly realizes, from Crosby's carefully controlled emotion, what living in that house has meant to Crosby. She kisses Crosby good-bye, and watches her, holding Rover on the leash, edge sideways down the slippery steps. "It was a dreadful moment; unhappy; muddled; altogether wrong. Crosby was so miserable; she was so glad. Yet as she held the door open her tears formed and fell." Maynard Keynes, who had been puzzled by *The Waves*, liked *The Years*, and thought this scene "beat" Chekhov's *Cherry Orchard* (*Diary*, April 4, 1937). There is the same pathos, the same sense of finality, the end of a phase of social history. But Mrs. Woolf is kinder to Crosby than Chekhov was to the old valet Firs, who is left behind, forgotten, in the old house.

Two other scenes may be singled out as deepening the impression, if not of the death, at least of the changing status, of the middle class; both occur early in the evening before the reunion, and both enrich the meaning of that gathering. Dr. Peggy Pargiter has come to pick up her old aunt Eleanor and take her across town to the party. As Eleanor, in an allusive and fragmentary fashion, recalls this or that from her own and the family past, Peggy thinks about old age and the endless avenues stretching back and the hundreds of doors that open and shut, before one can see what lies behind them; and she wishes Aunt Eleanor would talk more about her youth in that lost time that seems so interesting, safe, and unreal. Eleanor, on her part, is curious, too, about the viewpoint of the young, but the things she asks questions about seem to Peggy either as simple as two and two make four or so difficult that nobody in the world knows the answer. She is startled when Eleanor, glancing at the evening paper with a photo of a fat man shouting (Mussolini?), suddenly, in a rage, tears the paper and flings it to the floor, exclaiming, "Damned bully!" "It was the force that she had put into the words that impressed her, not the words. It was as if she still believed with passion—she, old Eleanor—in the things that man had destroyed. A wonderful generation, she thought, as they drove off. Believers.... 'You see,' Eleanor interrupted, as if she wanted to explain her words, 'it means the end of everything we cared for.' 'Freedom?' said Peggy perfunctorily. 'Yes,' said Eleanor. 'Freedom and justice.'" Peggy is perfunctory in her response, but the words sink in and color her mood at the party. During a lull she listens to the sounds of the London night: "a horn hooted; a siren wailed on the river. The far-away sounds, the suggestion they brought in of other worlds, indifferent to this world, of people toiling, grinding, in the heart of darkness, in the depths of night, made her say over Eleanor's words, Happy in this world, happy with living people. But how can one be 'happy,' she asked herself, in a world bursting with misery. On every placard at every street corner was Death; or worse—tyranny; brutality; torture; the fall of civilization; the end of freedom. We here, she thought, are only sheltering under a leaf, which will be destroyed."

Peggy's brother North, who had always kept up some connection with his odd cousin Sally, even when he was on his African farm, comes to have dinner with her in her sordid lodgings before they go to the party. The food, cooked in the basement and served by a slatternly maid, is underdone mutton and flyspecked fruit; one of those meals—like the mutton and prunes Mrs. Woolf had shared with the ladies at Cambridge—from which one shrinks. Sally's conversation with its picturesque exaggerations paints a picture of the London Waste Land—a polluted city, an unbelieving city, "city of dead fish and worn-out frying-pans"—she is thinking of a river's bank when the tide is out. She tells North how she had gone out to look for a job in the City, with a letter of introduction to a man who had been with her father at Oxford; and how she had paused at the bridge and watched the people passing—"the strutting; the tiptoeing; the pasty; the ferret-eyed; the bowler-hatted, servile innumerable army of workers. And I said, 'Must I join your conspiracy? Stain the hand, the unstained hand. . . .'" She is admitted to the luxurious private office of the man who had known her father—"a stout man with red cheeks. On his table three orchids in a vase. . . ." And so on. North wonders how much of it all is true, but the questions raised in his mind by Sally's mood remain with him during the evening, especially when,

feeling like an outsider, he listens to the young men talking
money and politics, manifestoes and meetings, Justice and
Liberty. What did they mean by these words, all these nice
young men with two or three hundred a year, and their
public school and college accents and tricks of speech? But
where—he looks around him at his aunt's guests—"where
are the Sweeps and the Sewer-men, the Seamstresses and the
Stevedores? he thought, making a list of trades that began
with the letter S. For all Delia's pride in her promiscuity, he
thought, glancing at the people, there were only Dons and
Duchesses, and what other words begin with D? . . . Drabs
and Drones?"

These questions are given too much prominence when
lifted out of the currents of memory, reflection, description,
and dialogue which flow through the evening. But in a subdued way they strike a note of profound anxiety which is
not sounded in Mrs. Woolf's earlier novels. As questions they
remain unanswered, like the questions about war in the 1917
interlude during the air raid; unanswered then, and now;
perhaps unanswerable. Unlike some of her younger contemporaries in the 1930's, Mrs. Woolf had no ready-made
answers and was the more vulnerable to anxiety because she
was "unprotected by the carapace of dogmatism," which
many of them possessed—as Ralph Bates pointed out, recalling a discussion among writers in 1936, of the role of the
artist in a crisis, when Mrs. Woolf was present.[18]

The Pargiters, then, are taken as a family from the middle-
class security of the later Victorian age to the threatening in-
stability of the decade before World War II. In this progression Mrs. Woolf has chosen the spring of 1914 to pause,
with Martin Pargiter, for a day and evening in London—at
a point of no return. Call it a "moment" in the life of London rather than in the life of Martin, though it is through
him that the experience comes to us. The day is brilliant,

18 Ralph Bates, New York *Herald Tribune Books*, Sept. 30, 1945.

the London season is beginning, the hour of eleven is proclaimed from the spires of all the churches, and Martin, in excellent spirits, decides to visit his stockbroker in the City, first walking from his Ebury Street lodgings to Hyde Park Corner and then rolling down Piccadilly in the bus to St. Paul's, where he indulges his architectural musings, and catches sight of his odd cousin Sally, prayer book in hand, coming out of the cathedral. He takes her for lunch to a chophouse frequented by his City friends; the food is excellent and so is the wine, which makes Sally embarrassingly talkative. Then they set out to meet Sally's sister Maggie and her baby at the Round Pond in Kensington. Mrs. Woolf, who finds the task of getting one's characters from luncheon to dinner a problem and presumably a bore, finds it a delight to get them from Fleet Street to Kensington Gardens. Sally and Martin on top of the bus are carried smoothly along Piccadilly past the Club windows where Colonel Pargiter used to sit. Entering the Park, they stroll first in the wrong direction and come to the "bald rubbed space" where speakers congregate and groups gather around orators on boxes and platforms. One speaker calls upon his fellow citizens to consider "Joostice and liberty," and bangs his fist on the rail of his platform. An old lady with a very small audience is saying something about sparrows. Turning away, they find the right path and see the Serpentine gleaming through the trees. The urbanity of the Park—Jacob had called a similar scene very urbane—pleased Martin, and the composition of water, trees, green slopes, curving drives, and strolling people made him feel like exchanging impressions with Sally, but Sally is talking to herself. They go past the open-air tea garden with its striped umbrellas and reach the Round Pond, where they join Maggie with her baby in its pram. Maggie and the baby were "dappled with lozenges of floating light." The scene that follows is a triumph of the Impressionist technique Mrs. Woolf first tried out in *Kew Gardens*; it is both

a Landscape with Figures and a Conversation Piece. While
Sally sleeps peacefully, her back against a tree, and the baby
sleeps in its pram, the long-separated cousins begin a des-
ultory conversation that grows more and more intimately
reminiscent as the tranquil beauty of the surroundings creates
an unusually harmonious mood. Mrs. Woolf wrote and rewrote this scene, wishing to "reduce it all so that each sentence, though perfectly natural dialogue, has a great pressure
of meaning behind it. And the most careful harmony and
contrast of scene . . . has also to be arranged" (*Diary*, Feb. 26,
1935). She achieved both. Light is thrown upon the family past, confidences exchanged. Martin tells her about his
father's mistress, whose letters he had found after his father's
death. Why had his father lied, he had thought at the time,
but then remembered some of the lies he himself had lived;
and family life had seemed to him an abominable system—
all those different people living in the same house, boxed up
together telling lies. But now, under the beneficent influence
of the time and place and the congenial company of his
cousin, the sting is drawn from that affair and also from his
own current difficulty with a possessive and jealous mistress.

The spell is broken when the baby wakes, and Martin
leaves them, to dress for dinner at his cousin's in Grosvenor
Square. The evening at Lady Lasswade's is as crowded with
impressions as his day had been, but his response is different,
his mood has changed; he feels detached and ill at ease,
especially with his young dinner companion whom he tries
unsuccessfully to impress. Everything is so correct—the
"right" people, the perfect hostess, the family portraits, the
footmen. Under the surface the two cousins carry on a sort
of duel, now and then expressed in a brief thrust and parry
of dialogue. There are shifts of viewpoint, back and forth, from
Martin to Lady Lasswade. Just as Clarissa Dalloway is un-
easily conscious that her old lover regards her life as full of
trivialities and herself as a snob, so Lady Lasswade is aware

that Martin is critical of the values of this society, so enclosed and so sure of itself, from old Lady Warburton to the youngest debutante, who after dinner sits on a stool at her feet. "Where's Timmy, Ann?" asks the old lady. "Harrow," replies Ann. "Ah, you've always been to Harrow," says the old lady, who knows the family traditions of all the right people. And then Lady Warburton, with the beautiful breeding that "simulated at least human charity," flatters the girl, likening her to her grandmother, a famous beauty. Ann, wishing to know more about her grandmother, hears from the old lady a selection from her memories—"an edition with asterisks"— "for it was a story that could hardly be told to a girl in white satin." Lady Warburton is one of the last to leave, and Martin, following her downstairs, watches her as she accepts her cloak with the violet slash in it from the footman, then her furs. "A bag dangled from her wrist. She was hung about with chains; her fingers were knobbed with rings. Her sharp stone-colored face, riddled with lines and wrinkled into creases, looked out from its soft nest of furs and laces. The eyes were still bright. The nineteenth century going to bed, Martin said to himself as he watched her hobble down the steps on the arm of her footman." An age is passing, a moment in the life of London.

IX

All great writers have "an atmosphere in which they seem most at their ease and at their best," wrote Mrs. Woolf in a review of Henry James's *Middle Years. Between the Acts,* her last novel, has her own distinctive atmosphere; the perspective is better adjusted to her own eyesight; whereas in *The Years* one feels that she is not always at her ease. The chronology tied her down to the clock ticking away through the decades; but the time in *Between the Acts* is Clarissa's, Mrs. Ramsay's, even Orlando's time. The past is caught in the present moment; not only the past of this and that character, but of a countryside and a literature. She wondered, after *The Years* was published, whether another novel would ever swim up; "the only hint I have towards it is that it's to be dialogue: and poetry: and prose; all quite distinct. No more closely written books" (*Diary*, Aug. 6, 1937). When the biography of Roger Fry was pressing heavily upon her during the following year, she amused herself with "Poyntz Hall: a centre: all literature discussed in connection with real little incongruous living humour: and anything that comes into my head.... And English country; and a scenic old house—and a terrace where nursemaids walk—and people passing—and a perpetual variety and change from intensity to prose" (April 26, 1938). She lived alternately in the "solid world of Roger and in the airy world of Poyntz Hall" (May 20, 1938). Recognizing that she sometimes overdid the lyric vein in prose, she let that vein run off into poems. And there is plenty of opportunity to break out into verse in the pageant that is acted out on a June day in 1939 on the grounds of Poyntz Hall, the home of the Olivers. The spectators are the Olivers themselves and their guests, and the neighboring gentry; the actors are the villagers—surprisingly transformed by their roles; and the creator and director of the pageant of English history is Miss La Trobe, a writer of plays, living in the village. She belongs with the artists in Mrs. Woolf's world, seeking not so much—like Lily Briscoe—to express her inner vision as to reach the imagination of her audience, and thinking in moments of frustration, "O to write a play without an audience—*the* play!"

But the audience is a part of the play; and Miss La Trobe herself makes it so in the last scene—"The Present Time: Ourselves"—when by an ingenious manipulation of mirrors in the hands of the chorus the audience looks at itself, to its bewilderment and discomfiture. Both audience and actors— the Olivers and their guests, their servants, the neighboring

gentry, and the villagers from the parson to the village idiot—
are all part of the history of England during the twenty-four
hours encompassed by the novel. And it is a novel, odd as the
pattern is, because it has characters, and they have changing
relationships, and the leading ones have pasts—those caves
scooped out behind the present, as Mrs. Woolf thought of
them when she was writing *Mrs. Dalloway*—and they live
those twenty-four hours in surroundings that are a part of
their past and their present. Mrs. Woolf never did a more
beautiful job in integrating the parts of her design than in
this brief book. It offers a temptation to critics fond of
analogies between the arts; in this case it would probably be
music; and it would be relevant, in studying the development
of Mrs. Woolf's art, to look back twenty years to her *String
Quartet*, for a theme capable—as *Between the Acts* proves
—of fascinating variations and combinations with other
themes.

While she was writing *The Years*, Mrs. Woolf referred in
her *Diary* to "upper air scenes." Most of the scenes in *Between the Acts* are upper air scenes; social comedy scenes in
the drawing room and dining room of the Oliver house; during the intervals in the performance of the pageant, especially
the tea interval in the great barn; and the pageant itself is
comedy and often hilarious, at that. But it isn't all upper air
nor all comedy. An ominous note is struck when Giles
Oliver, escaping for a few moments from the crowd and
brooding over the dangerous international situation, crushes
with his foot a snake choking on a toad it can't quite swallow,
and smears his tennis shoe with blood—a sinister little symbol. Just below the surface trouble threatens, as a little drama
develops between young Mrs. Oliver—Isa—and one of the
guests, a gentleman farmer, who briefly excites her interest,
partly because relations with her husband are strained and
Isa is romantic and the gentleman farmer has a ravaged face
and she suspects passion and mystery. Tags of romantic

poetry float along in her stream of consciousness; they fit in nicely with the verses in the pageant. Another little drama develops between Giles and an unexpected guest at luncheon —Mrs. Manresa, a nonintellectual, intuitive child of Nature, as this potentially predatory lady likes to think of herself among the Intellectuals. Mrs. Manresa is the only one in the audience who is not embarrassed at all by the mirror trick, but promptly seizes the opportunity to repair her make-up. This little affair, so far as we know, comes to nothing. But when the day is over and Giles and Isa are alone with their jealousies, they quarrel. "Alone, enmity was bared; also love. Before they slept, they must fight; after they fought, they would embrace. From that embrace another life might be born." After the sophistication of the highly civilized upper air scenes of that day, they are alone with primitive emotions. The window of their room shows all sky without color. "The house had lost its shelter. It was night before roads were made, or house. It was the night that dwellers in caves had watched from some high place among rocks. Then the curtain rose. They spoke."

A similar note, suggesting the long past, is struck at the beginning, late in the evening in the drawing room, by old Mr. Oliver, of the Indian Civil Service, retired, talking with his guests about the plan of the county council to bring water to the village. The site chosen for the cesspool is on the Roman road, easy to see from an airplane; and one could see the scars made by the Britons, and later by the Elizabethan manor house, and by the plow, when they plowed the hill to grow wheat during the Napoleonic Wars. This sense of time past is in the mind of his sister, old Mrs. Swithin, when she wakes the next morning, having read late in her favorite *Outline of History*. She was thinking of the rhododendron forests in Piccadilly, when the Continent, not yet divided by a channel, was still all one, and populated by elephant-bodied, seal-necked, heaving, surging, slowly writhing, and, she supposed, barking monsters, "from whom presumably, she thought, jerking the window open, we descend." No wonder she jumped when Grace came in with the breakfast tray. " 'Batty,' Grace called her, as she felt on her face a divided glance that was half meant for a beast in a swamp, half for a maid in a print frock and white apron." "Mrs. Swithin was given to increasing the bounds of the moment by flights into past or future; or sidelong down corridors and alleys." So is Mrs. Swithin's creator; and old Mrs. Swithin is one of Mrs. Woolf's happiest creations; sitting down to morning tea, "like any other old lady with a high nose, thin cheeks, a ring on her finger and the usual trappings of rather shabby but gallant old age, which included in her case a cross gleaming gold on her breast." For she belongs to the unifiers; she seeks some order and meaning in the history of humanity, and wrestles with the problem in a bewildering feminine way that is an affront to the logical mind of her brother, who belongs to the separatists. But there is deep affection, if little understanding, between them.

The barn, where Mrs. Swithin goes later in the morning to see if things are in order for the afternoon tea, is much older than the house; "as old as the church, and built of the same stone, but it had no steeple. It was raised on cones of grey stone at the corners to protect it from rats and damp. . . . The roof was weathered red-orange; and inside it was a hollow hall, sun-shafted, smelling of corn, dark when the doors were shut, but splendidly illuminated when the doors at the end stood open, as they did to let the wagons in—the long low wagons, like ships of the sea, breasting the corn, not the sea, returning in the evening shagged with hay." The barn, when empty of human beings, has a life of its own: "Mice slid in and out of holes, or stood upright, nibbling. Swallows were busy with straw in pockets of earth in the rafters. Countless beetles and insects of various sorts burrowed in the dry wood. A stray bitch had made the dark corner where the sacks stood a lying-in ground for her puppies. All these eyes, expanding and narrowing, some adapted to the light, others to darkness, looked from different angles and edges. Minute nibblings and rustlings broke the silence. Whiffs of sweetness and richness veined the air. A blue-bottle had settled on the cake and stabbed its yellow rock with its short drill. A butterfly sunned itself sensuously on a sunlit yellow plate."

The barn fills up with human beings: Mrs. Sands the cook and her helpers preparing the tea and sandwiches, the village girls and young men decorating it with garlands of paper roses left over from the Coronation, and Mrs. Swithin (known as Old Flimsy in the village) nailing a placard on the door, to replace one torn down by the village idiot. "The old girl, with a wisp of white hair flying, knobbed shoes as if she had claws corned like a canary's, and black stockings wrinkled over the ankles, naturally made David cock his eye and Jessica wink back, as she handed him a length of paper roses. Snobs they were; long enough stationed that is in that one corner of the world to have taken indelibly the print of some three hundred years of customary behaviour. So they laughed; but respected. If she wore pearls, pearls they were." Bond, the cowman, stopped at the door and contemplated the young people. "He thought very little of anybody, simples or gentry. Leaning, silent, sardonic, against the door, he was like a withered willow, bent over a stream, all its leaves shed, and in his eyes the whimsical flow of the waters."

Village festivals are in the tradition of the countryside. Nowadays, as Mr. Oliver explains, they all end up with a demand for money; this time the collection will go into the fund for installing electricity in the church. One year, Mrs. Swithin explains, they gave *Gammer Gurton's Needle* and another time they wrote the play themselves; and for the pageant, there is the whole of English literature to choose from. The prologue is spoken by a little girl—"England am

I." Offstage the gramophone chuffs, chuffs through the scenes. An older girl speaks for England in the time of Chaucer, and behind her passes a procession through the trees of the Canterbury pilgrims. "Merrie England," comments Mrs. Manresa, and reflects that it would take till midnight unless they skipped a few centuries. Next comes an Elizabethan play, a skillful parody, almost good enough to be true—with a false duke, a princess disguised as a boy, an old crone who saves the rightful heir, who turns out to be the beggar, identified by a mole on his cheek. But the plot did not matter—"the plot was only there to beget emotion"—incidentally, Mrs. Woolf's own opinion about plots. Lovers are married, secrets disclosed. The verses quite shamelessly borrow or distort lines from Elizabethan drama. It all ends up with a riotous dance of dukes, priests, shepherds, servingmen, around the commanding figure of Queen Elizabeth, personified by Mrs. Clark, "licensed to sell tobacco" in the village. "It didn't matter what the words were; or who sang what. Round and round they whirled, intoxicated by the music." Then a procession formed and great Eliza descended from her soapbox, and "taking her skirts in her hand, striding with long strides surrounded by Dukes and Princes, followed by the lovers arm in arm, with Albert the idiot playing in and out, and the corpse on its bier concluding the procession, the Elizabethan age passed from the scene," to great applause from the audience. Orlando's progress through English literature is decorous by comparison.

As the audience scatters for the intermission, Miss La Trobe wonders if she can ever get them together again; "every moment the audience slipped the noose; split up into scraps and fragments." Had she made them see? No, another failure. They drift off. Isa shows William Dodge, the unhappy odd man, the greenhouse; it is a nice place for couples to explore relationships; during the next interval, Giles takes Mrs. Manresa there. But soon strains from the gramophone announce the next scene, and Mabel Hopkins, statuesque in a gray satin robe (a bedspread), pinned in stonelike folds, makes her entrance, carrying a scepter and an orb—Queen Anne or the Age of Reason. Mrs. Elmhurst reads the program aloud for the benefit of her husband; another play, *Where there's a Will there's a Way.* And the characters—Lady Harpy Harraden, Sir Spaniel Lilyliver, Lord and Lady Fribble—what names! "Out they came from the bushes—men in flowered waistcoats, white waistcoats and buckled shoes; women wearing brocades tucked up, hooped and draped; glass stars, blue ribands and imitation pearls made them look the very image of Lords and Ladies." The play is an entertaining burlesque of Restoration drama, with its witty, corrupt, intriguing and double-dealing fops and ladies of fashion.

The gramophone, while the scene shifts into the nineteenth century, gently states certain facts, in a Gray's *Elegy* sort of manner, about Eve letting her dewy mantle fall, and the good wife on the table spreading her simple fare, and the shepherds fluting and herding the flocks—all in keeping with the cooling air and the setting sun. Winding in and out among the trees in the background a chorus of villagers sing of the root-life of the countryside, the passing of the seasons, digging and delving, while Babylon and Troy, Agamemnon and Caesar pass away. During a pause the cows take up the burden, started off by one who bellows, having lost her calf; then they all bellow, yearning—"the primeval voice sounding loud in the ear of the present moment."

Introducing the Victorian age, a "huge symbolical figure emerged from the bushes. It was Budge the publican; but so disguised that even cronies who drank with him nightly failed to recognize him. . . . He wore a long black many-caped cloak; waterproof; shiny; of the substance of a statue in Parliament Square; a helmet which suggested a policeman; a row of medals crossed his breast; and in his right hand he held extended a special constable's baton (loaned by Mr.

Willert of the Hall)." He directs the traffic at Hyde Park
Corner, and intones the laws of God and Man, engrossed
on a sheet of parchment. It only wanted a shower of rain,
a flight of pigeons, the pealing bells of St. Paul's to "transport
them to a foggy London afternoon, with the muffin bells
ringing and the church bells pealing at the very height of
Victorian prosperity." But the older ladies are disturbed by a
slightly sneering tone, aimed somehow at their fathers—for
"there were grand men among them." As the scene shifts
to a Victorian family picnic party, and the gramophone
provides once-popular songs and London street cries, memories are stirred and an obbligato of comments from the
older ladies fills in the pauses. A song reminds one of crinolines and stays and many petticoats—unhygienic no doubt—
look at my daughter, "forty but slim as a wand." Perhaps
even the Victorian home—a cozy little set, of a lamplit room
and ruby curtains and papa reading aloud—was unhygienic,
muses Mrs. Lynn Jones, the old widow of the Mount, or why
had it perished? Time went on and on like the hands of a
clock, and if they met with no resistance, they would still be
going round and round. "The Home would have remained;
and Papa's beard, she thought, would have grown and grown;
and Mama's knitting—what did she do with all her knitting?
—Change had to come ... or there'd have been yards and
yards of Papa's beard, of Mama's knitting. . . . Dear, how my
mind wanders, she checked herself." " 'Were they like that?'
Isa asked abruptly. She looked at Mrs. Swithin as if she had
been a dinosaur or a very diminutive mammoth. Extinct she
must be, since she had lived in the reign of Queen Victoria.
. . . 'The Victorians,' Mrs. Swithin mused. 'I don't believe,'
she said with her odd little smile, 'that there ever were such
people. Only you and me and William dressed differently.' "

Before the Victorian scene, Mrs. Swithin pokes her head
through the bushes that screen the actors' dressing room, to
congratulate Miss La Trobe. " 'You've given me ... Ever

since I was a child I've felt...' A film fell over her eyes,
shutting off the present. She tried to recall her childhood;
then gave it up; and, with a little wave of her hand, as if
asking Miss La Trobe to help her out, continued: 'This daily
round; this going up and down stairs...' She gazed at Miss
La Trobe with a cloudless old-aged stare. Their eyes met in
a common effort to bring a common meaning to birth. They
failed; and Mrs. Swithin, laying hold desperately of a fraction
of her meaning, said, 'What a small part I've had to play!
But you've made me feel I could have played...Cleo-
patra.'" She meant, Miss La Trobe reflected, "you've stirred
in me my unacted part." As she tied the tapes of the
voluminous gown she was helping Mrs. Rogers to put on,
"'You've twitched the invisible strings,' was what the old
lady meant; and revealed—of all people—Cleopatra!" For a
moment glory possessed her.

After the brief shower that rescues the pageant from a
dragging moment, and after the scene "Ourselves," with
mirrors, a voice speaks out of the bushes through a mega-
phone, pointing a moral—all you see of yourselves is scraps,
orts, fragments—and then the gramophone mercifully plays
—Bach? Beethoven? Mozart?—uniting the distracted minds;
and then Mr. Streatfield, the clergyman, makes a brave effort
at interpreting a puzzling pageant—"we act different parts?
but are the same? I leave it to you"—and continues speaking
in his familiar capacity as treasurer of the fund, pointing out
that there is still a deficit; whereupon collecting boxes appear
by magic. Finally "God Save the King," and dispersal, actors
still in their costumes mingling with the audience, scattered
dialogue and comment, local gossip, and the gramophone's
valedictory—"Dispersed are we who have come together."
Miss La Trobe gathers up her records; she had given her gift
—it was in the giving that the triumph was; she is depressed
and seeks forgetfulness in the local pub; but before we leave
her, the first words of a new play are beginning to shape

themselves. There is a little interchange between Mrs. Swithin and her brother beside the lily pond; they disagree as usual; "he would carry the torch of reason till it went out in the darkness of the cave. For herself, every morning, kneeling, she protected her vision." The family is alone at last, the post and the next morning's paper are brought in— "the paper that obliterated the day before." Each thinks his own thoughts, before separating for the night. "Bartholomew flicked on the reading lamp. The circle of the readers, attached to white papers, was lit up. There in that hollow of the sun-baked field were congregated the grasshopper, the ant, and the beetle, rolling pebbles of sun-baked earth through the glistening stubble. In that rosy corner of the sun-baked field Bartholomew, Giles and Lucy polished and nibbled and broke off crumbs. Isa watched them." The curtain falls on the scene, already referred to, between Isa and Giles. The interval "between the acts"—between two world wars--had ended.

4. Toward a Conclusion

IF A COLLECTED EDITION of Virginia Woolf's letters is ever published—and one wishes she could review it for the *TLS*, if it is—opinions and conclusions about her art will no doubt undergo revision. Meanwhile the critic does what he can with the published extracts from her *Diary*, the letters that have been printed in books and articles, the reminiscences of her friends—anything that throws light on how she worked and what she thought about her own writings. The owners of unpublished letters permit quotations from time to time. The following extracts are from letters in the possession of Miss Daphne Sanger, written by Mrs. Woolf to Miss Sanger's father, Charles Percy Sanger, a barrister, about whom Mr. Leonard Woolf has an interesting footnote in his autobiography, *Sowing* (p. 201).* Mr. Sanger wrote to Mrs. Woolf about several of her novels, soon after their publication. Replying on October 30, 1922, from Hogarth House, Richmond, to some comments about *Jacob's Room*, Mrs. Woolf wrote: "I think a close study of *Jacob's Room*, should you ever wish to approach the book again, will reveal many passages which a trained mind would have pinched

* They are published here with the permission of Miss Sanger and Mr. Woolf.

much closer together; and others where the mistakes are glaring. What about lilacs in April, fountains in Neville's Court, tulips in August, etc. I am not going to pick them all out for your benefit. What I do feel is that education helps one to be drastic with oneself, instead of sloppy: But—as age increases I do more and more believe in thought as an element of fiction. You are quite right, I am sure, in having grave doubts about the form of *Jacob's Room*. So have I. It would take too long to explain why I had this time to use it, and what I hope next time to do with it. . . . But as you ought to know, I have a humble respect, not to say veneration, for your judgment, and so if you found good in it, I am immediately encouraged." Soon after *Mrs. Dalloway* appeared, Mr. Sanger wrote again, and Mrs. Woolf replied, from Tavistock Square, May 26 (no year): "It is extremely good of you to write and tell me what you think of *Mrs. Dalloway* and your views interest me enormously. I expect you are right about the lack of sympathy, but in self-defence I must remark that I think the queerness of the method is partly responsible for your feeling this. I think, at least, that at first go off it is much easier to get the technical qualities of an experiment than to get any emotion from it." (Some comments on Chekhov, evidently in answer to Mr. Sanger, follow.) Then the letter goes on: "Indeed, the reason why I inflict these experiments upon you is that I can't lie down in peace until I have found some way of liberating my sympathies instead of giving effect to my analytic brain. But the conditions make it very hard for a novelist to do this now— in England at any rate. But come and see us, and let us argue the question by word of mouth."

May 17, 1927, she replied to Mr. Sanger's letter about *To the Lighthouse*: "You are amazing in the way you read your friends' books. It is the greatest encouragement. I can't say how glad I am that you like the *Lighthouse*. You said Mrs. Dalloway lacked humanity; and if this is better in that way, it is a proof that I took your strictures to heart. I confess I sometimes want to cut the whole psychology business altogether; it is so endless, but I get drawn in against my wish. Those jumps and jolts you complain of are not at all to my liking. Unfortunately one is doing a very difficult thing with imperfect means. I can never scrape through a book without disaster."

Some of the self-criticism expressed in these letters is to be found in A *Writer's Diary*. Mrs. Woolf was always aware of the gap between her intention and her achievement, and always bent upon further experiment. Several passages in these letters, however, deserve comment. What did she mean by coming to believe more and more in "thought as an element in fiction"? What was the problem of liberating her sympathies instead of giving effect to her analytic brain? And what were the conditions that made this difficult for a novelist, just then, in England? Why did she want to cut the "whole psychology business"? Some answers are suggested in two articles published in the New York *Herald Tribune Books*, August 14 and 21, 1927, and reprinted as "The Narrow Bridge of Art" in *Granite and Rainbow*. Mrs. Woolf the critic often clarified and formulated the problems of Mrs. Woolf the novelist. The subject of the articles is indicated in the original title, "Poetry, Fiction, and the Future." The "modern mind"—the mind seeking literary expression—finds the old tools, lyric poetry and poetic drama, inadequate to deal with the world of the 1920's. "The mind is full of monstrous, hybrid, unmanageable emotions. That the age of the earth is 3,000,000,000 years; that human life lasts but a second; that the capacity of the human mind is nevertheless boundless; that life is infinitely beautiful but repulsive; that one's fellow creatures are adorable but disgusting; that science and religion have between them destroyed belief; that all bonds of union seem broken, yet some control must exist—it is in this atmosphere of doubt and conflict that writers have now to create." Characteristic of the modern mind is the strange way in which things that have no apparent connection are associated; "feelings which used to come single and separate do so no longer. Beauty is part ugliness; amusement part disgust; pleasure part pain. Emotions which used to enter the mind whole are now broken up on the threshold. For example: It is a spring night, the moon is up, the nightingale singing, the willows bending over the river. Yes, but at the same time a diseased old woman is picking over her greasy rags on a hideous iron bench. She and the spring enter his mind together; they blend but do not mix." Incongruous emotions are coupled together. In Keats's *Ode to a Nightingale* "sorrow is the shadow which accompanies beauty. In the modern mind beauty is accompanied not by its shadow but by its opposite. The modern poet talks of the nightingale who sings 'jug jug to dirty ears.'" Troubled by discords, incongruities, skepticism, a testing spirit, sneering at beauty for being beautiful, unable to accept anything simply for what it is—the modern mind is in the Waste Land, afflicted with that "dissociation of sensibility" made familiar to us by T. S. Eliot. Surely this is one explanation of what Mrs. Woolf meant by the difficulty of liberating her sympathies from her analytic brain.

Speculation about the duties, once discharged by poetry, which prose will eventually take over, leads of course to "that cannibal, the novel," and to what it may be expected to give us. We already know (from the "Mr. Bennett and Mrs. Brown" essay) that it will have "little kinship with the sociological novel or the novel of environment." "It will resemble poetry in this that it will give not only or mainly people's relations to each other and their activities together, as the novel has hitherto done, but it will give the relation of the mind to general ideas and its soliloquy in solitude. For under the dominion of the novel we have scrutinized one part of the mind closely and left another unexplored. . . . We forget that we spend much time sleeping, dreaming, thinking, reading, alone; we are not entirely occupied in personal relations; all our energies are not absorbed in making our livings. The psychological novelist has been too prone to limit psychology to the psychology of personal intercourse; we long sometimes to escape from the incessant, the remorseless analysis of falling into love and falling out of love. . . . We long for some more impersonal relationship. We long for ideas, for dreams, for imaginations, for poetry." Here is the impatience with some aspects of the "psychology business" and the desire to have more thought in fiction.

Consider "thought" in her own fiction. The people in her fictional world may reason when they think, especially if they are men, but men or women, their thinking is colored by their feeling. What it feels like to think is an experience to be recorded, just as significant as what it feels like to be in love or to lose a friend. In her earlier novels Mrs. Woolf often tells us, in the convention of the traditional novel, what her characters are thinking. Mrs. Ambrose, in *The Voyage Out*, for instance, reflects upon what she has been observing of the life in the resort hotel: "The little jokes, the chatter, the inanities of the afternoon had shrivelled up before her eyes. Underneath the likings and spites, the comings together and partings, great things were happening—terrible things because they were so great. Her sense of safety was shaken, as if beneath twigs and dead leaves she had seen the movements of a snake. It seemed to her that a moment's respite was allowed, a moment's make-believe, and then again the profound and reasonless law asserted itself, moulding them all to its liking, making and destroying." A dozen years later Mrs. Ramsay—the perfected portrait that is foreshadowed in Mrs. Ambrose—comes to much the same conclusion, but not by the path of conscious reflection. Sitting by the window, knitting or putting together the pictures her son had been cutting out or glancing from time to time at her husband as he passes back and forth along the terrace—and Mr. Ramsay is engaged in the proper masculine kind of thinking about his philosophical work—Mrs. Ramsay finds it pleasant to be alone, not to have to think, to be herself, "a wedge-shaped core of darkness, something invisible to others.... When life sank down for a moment, the range of experience seemed limitless." She indulges herself in dreaming about all the places she has not seen. "This core of darkness could go anywhere, for no one saw it.... Not as oneself did one find rest ever, in her experience (she accomplished here something dexterous with her needles) but as a wedge of darkness. Losing personality, one lost the fret, the hurry, the stir." She feels a sense of triumph over life, and, pausing, looks out to meet the stroke of the lighthouse, "the long steady stroke, the last of the three, which was her stroke." Often as she watches like this, the light lifts up some little phrase that had been lying in her mind; this time she finds herself thinking, "We are in the hands of the Lord." "The insincerity slipping in among the truths roused her, annoyed her. She returned to her knitting again. How could any Lord have made this world? she asked. With her mind she had always seized the fact that there is no reason, order, justice: but suffering, death, the poor. There was no treachery too base for the world to commit; she knew that. No happiness lasted; she knew that." As she knits, she looks so stern that "when her husband passed, though he was chuckling at the thought that Hume, the philosopher, grown enormously fat, had stuck in a bog, he could not help noting, as he passed, the sternness at the heart of her beauty." Moments after, stopping her knitting, she looks again at the beam from the lighthouse, "hypnotised, as if it were stroking with its silver fingers some sealed vessel in her brain, whose bursting would flood her with delight." She has after all known happiness. "The beam silvered the rough waves a little more brightly, as daylight faded, and the blue went out of the sea and it rolled in waves of pure lemon which curved and swelled and broke upon the beach and the ecstasy burst in her eyes and waves of pure delight raced over the floor of her mind."

Mrs. Woolf, in the words of Bernard Blackstone, "explored the world of the mind—especially the feminine mind—under precise conditions of character and environment." [1] Mr. Ramsay is at times enraged by the folly of women's minds. But Mrs. Ramsay feels that to pursue truth with the astonishing lack of consideration for other people's feelings that Mr. Ramsay sometimes shows is to rend the thin veils of civilization, to commit a horrible outrage on human decency. It would not be Mrs. Ramsay who would "carry the torch of reason till it went out in the darkness of the cave." It is old Mr. Oliver (in *Between the Acts*) who would do that. But Virginia Woolf was not Mrs. Ramsay. It has been pointed out that, though she shared some concepts of time with Bergson, she did not share the Bergsonian revolt against reason. "She observes the stream of consciousness, but she examines it with an intellectual instrument in which she, unlike many contemporary writers, has not lost her faith"— as Winifred Holtby pointed out in her brilliant little book on Virginia Woolf. Perhaps, Miss Holtby speculated, it was her early readings in Greek that led her to believe in "the validity of the intellectual approach to truth." [2] E. M. Forster speaks of her exquisite and catholic senses—"she reminds us of the importance of sensation in an age which practises brutality and recommends ideals." But after the senses, the intellect. "She respected knowledge, she believed in wisdom. Though she could not be called an optimist, she had, very profoundly, the conviction that mind is in action against matter, and is winning new footholds in the void." She cared for the abstractions—Order, Justice, Truth—and tried to express them

1 Bernard Blackstone, *Virginia Woolf*, 1952.
2 Winifred Holtby, *Virginia Woolf*, 1932.

through such symbols as Rhoda, in *The Waves*, built out of the music of Mozart—the square upon the oblong. Mr. Forster concluded his Rede Lecture: "Sometimes it is as a row of little silver cups that I see her work gleaming. 'These trophies,' the inscription runs, 'were won by the mind from matter, its enemy and its friend.'"

The symbol of her faith—and it is a matter of regret to some of her critics—is not the dome of St. Paul's but the dome of the British Museum. When in the 1922 letter to Mr. Sanger she expressed her belief in "thought" in fiction, she had already written the eloquent passages in *Jacob's Room* about the light shining from Cambridge and about that "vast mind sheeted with stone," the British Museum. They are easy to excerpt for quotation, but it is not easy in the later novels to quote out of context examples of "thought." Thought and feeling became much more deeply interfused. Try separating Mrs. Ramsay's or Mrs. Swithin's thinking from her feeling.

It was in an apologetic mood, after the gay adventure of *Orlando*, that Mrs. Woolf wrote to Mr. Sanger that her books sometimes seemed to her to have no bearing on anything that is really happening. With this opinion some recent criticism is quite in accord. What, after all, are Mrs. Woolf's characters up to? Nothing very important: Mrs. Ramsay sits at a window knitting and presides over a dinner table; Miss La Trobe puts on a rather absurd pageant; Lily Briscoe paints a picture; Jacob sails a boat and sleeps with a prostitute; Mrs. Dalloway gives a party, and Mr. Dalloway buys roses for his wife; Septimus Smith jumps out the window; Orlando functions as an ambassador and changes his sex; and so on. Are these people socially responsible? Did Mrs. Woolf neglect to place them within the social framework "in which human hopes and despairs must be viewed," if they are to have meaning? The phrase quoted is from an article by Angus Wilson in the *TLS*, "Diversity and Depth," August 15, 1958, in which he laid stress upon the seriousness of the best Victorian fiction, which made it adult reading for responsible men and women. "It is surely," he writes, "the belief that the 'experimental' or 'Bloomsbury' novelists had erred in departing from this sort of seriousness that has more than anything else determined the general trend of post-war English novelists towards a return to the traditional forms. No sharpening of visual image, no increased sensibility, no deeper penetration of the individual consciousness, whether by verbal experiment or by Freudian analysis, could fully atone for the frivolity of ignoring man as a social being, for treating personal relationships and subjective sensations in a social void." He adds that this is an exaggerated and false picture "even of the novels of Virginia Woolf." But her very genius singles her out for attack. Later in the article he expresses the belief that breadth of setting, essential to an "adult" statement, has involved the sacrifice of depth of vision. "Without in any way departing from my adherence to the post-war social novel, I fear that the central characters are inferior in reality and depth to Mrs. Woolf's, though their problems and values seem to me of greater significance." Mr. Wilson includes his own characters in this criticism.

The novelist of today, of any day, seeking to communicate what he considers most significant, must experiment as Mrs. Woolf experimented, fashioning new tools, and reshaping or renouncing old ones, for you cannot, as she said, "cross the narrow bridge of art carrying all its tools in your hands. Some you must leave behind." [3] She believed that any method was right, every method was right, that expressed "what we wish to express, if we are writers; that brings us closer to the novelist's intention, if we are readers." [4] Life itself is the perpetual challenge to the novelist, life which is "always and

---

3 "The Narrow Bridge of Art," in *Granite and Rainbow*, p. 22.
4 "Modern Fiction," in *The Common Reader* I.

inevitably much richer than we who try to express it." [5] In her own experiments, far as they led her, she "never lost sight of her human responsibility as an artist to communicate with her fellow creatures, never allowed herself to stray off arrogantly into a private world, never willingly left her meaning obscure." [6]

One of the last entries in *A Writer's Diary*, October 12, 1940, records a happy day at Rodmell: "If it were not treasonable to say so, a day like this is almost too—I won't say happy: but amenable. The tune varies, from one nice melody to another. All is played (today) in such a theatre. Hills and fields; I can't stop looking; October blooms; brown plough; and the fading and freshening of the marsh. Now the mist comes up. And one thing's pleasant after another: breakfast, writing, walking, tea, bowls, reading, sweets, bed. A letter from Rose about her day. I let it almost break mine. Mine recovers. The globe rounds again."

5 *Granite and Rainbow*, p. 23.
6 "Virginia Woolf," *Time and Tide*, April 12, 1941.

Bibliography

I

Chronological list of the works of Virginia Woolf.
Unless otherwise indicated, the dates are of the first
London edition.

The Voyage Out	1915
The Mark on the Wall	1917
Night and Day	1919
Kew Gardens	1919
An Unwritten Novel	1920
Monday or Tuesday	1921
Jacob's Room	1922
Mr. Bennett and Mrs. Brown	1924
The Common Reader: First Series	1925
Mrs. Dalloway	1925
To the Lighthouse	1927
"Street Haunting: A London Adventure" (Yale Review)	1927
Orlando	1928
A Room of One's Own	1929
On Being Ill	1930
The Waves	1931
Letter to a Young Poet	1932
The Common Reader: Second Series	1932
Flush	1933

Walter Sickert: A Conversation   1934
The Years   1937
Three Guineas   1938
Reviewing   1939
Roger Fry: A Biography   1940
Between the Acts   1941
The Death of the Moth and Other Essays   1942
A Haunted House and Other Short Stories   1944
The Moment and Other Essays   1947
The Captain's Death Bed and Other Essays   1950
A Writer's Diary (Extracts from the Diary of Virginia
    Woolf, edited by Leonard Woolf)   1953
Virginia Woolf and Lytton Strachey: Letters   1956
Granite and Rainbow: Essays   1958

For a complete bibliography, see A *Bibliography of Virginia
    Woolf*, by B. J. Kirkpatrick. London: Rupert Hart-Davis,
    1957.

A uniform edition of the works of Virginia Woolf is pub-
    lished by the Hogarth Press, London. In the United
    States, the publisher is Harcourt, Brace & Co.

                                 II

A selected list of books and articles about Virginia Woolf.

BENNETT, JOAN. *Virginia Woolf, Her Art as a Novelist.* Cam-
    bridge University Press, 1945.
BLACKSTONE, BERNARD. *Virginia Woolf: A Commentary.* New
    York: Harcourt, Brace & Co., 1949.
———. *Virginia Woolf.* London: Longmans, Green & Co.,
    1952. Includes an alphabetical list of essays and stories.
BREWSTER, DOROTHY. *Virginia Woolf's London.* London:
    G. Allen & Unwin, 1959; New York: New York Univer-
    sity Press, 1960.
CHAMBERS, R. L. *The Novels of Virginia Woolf.* Edinburgh:
    Oliver & Boyd, 1947.

DAICHES, DAVID. *Virginia Woolf*. Norfolk, Conn.: New Directions Books, 1942.

DELATTRE, F. *Le Roman psychologique de Virginia Woolf*. Paris, 1932. Interesting section on "la durée bergsonienne."

FORSTER, E. M. *Virginia Woolf: The Rede Lecture*. Cambridge University Press, 1942; New York: Harcourt, Brace & Co., 1942.

GUIGUET, JEAN. *Virginia Woolf et son œuvre*. Paris: Didier, 1962.

HAFLEY, JAMES. *The Glass Roof: Virginia Woolf as Novelist*. University of California Press, 1954. Includes list of foreign reviews and criticism.

HOLTBY, WINIFRED. *Virginia Woolf*. London: Wishart & Co., 1932.

Horizon, May and June, 1941. Articles by T. S. Eliot, Duncan Grant, Rose Macaulay, William Plomer, and V. Sackville-West.

ISHERWOOD, CHRISTOPHER. "Virginia Woolf," *Decision*, May, 1941.

NATHAN, MONIQUE. *Virginia Woolf*. Trans. by Herma Briffault. New York: Evergreen Profile Book, Grove Press, Inc., 1961. Includes a short anthology of writings by Virginia Woolf, and over 80 photographs of people and places.

PIPPETT, AILEEN. *The Moth and the Star: A Biography of Virginia Woolf*. Boston: Little, Brown & Co., 1955. Contains extensive quotations from Virginia Woolf's letters to V. Sackville-West over the period from 1922 to 1941.

Time and Tide, "Virginia Woolf," April 12, 1941.

III

A selected list of books and articles, containing biographical and/or critical references to Virginia Woolf; quotations from her letters; extracts from her writings.

ANNAN, NOEL. *Leslie Stephen, His Thought and Character in Relation to His Time.* London: Macgibbon & Kee, 1951.

BELL, CLIVE. *Old Friends: Personal Recollections.* London: Chatto & Windus, 1956.

BREWSTER, DOROTHY. *East-West Passage: A Study in Literary Relationships.* London: G. Allen & Unwin, Ltd., 1954. Pp. 206–208, 223.

Cambridge Scrapbook, A. Collected by Jean Lindsay. Enlarged edition. Cambridge: W. Heffer & Sons, 1960. Contains extracts from *A Room of One's Own* and *Jacob's Room,* and other impressions of Cambridge by Sir Leslie Stephen, G. L. Dickinson, E. M. Forster, J. M. Keynes, C. Isherwood, etc.

CAMERON, JULIA MARGARET. *Victorian Photographs.* With introductions by Virginia Woolf and Roger Fry. London: Hogarth Press, 1926.

CLIFFORD, JAMES L. (ed.) *Biography as an Art,* Selected Criticism 1560–1960. New York: Oxford University Press, 1962. Pp. 126–34.

CLUTTON-BROCK, ALAN. "Vanessa Bell and Her Circle," *Listener,* May 4, 1961.

DAICHES, DAVID. *The Novel and the Modern World.* University of Chicago Press, Rev. ed., 1960. Chapter X.

GARNETT, DAVID. *The Flowers of the Forest.* London: Chatto & Windus, 1955. Pp. 160–62 and *passim.*

JOHNSTONE, J. K. *The Bloomsbury Group.* A study of E. M. Forster, Lytton Strachey, Virginia Woolf, and their circle. London: Secker & Warburg, 1954.

KRONENBERGER, LOUIS. "Virginia Woolf as Critic," *The Republic of Letters—Essays on Various Writers.* New York: A. A. Knopf, 1955.

LEHMANN, JOHN. *The Open Night.* London: Longmans, Green & Co., 1952; New York: Harcourt, Brace & Co., 1952. Pp. 23–33.

———. *The Whispering Gallery.* London: Longmans, Green & Co., 1955. Pp. 167–72.

LEHMANN, JOHN. "Working with Virginia Woolf," *Listener*, Jan. 13, 1955.

———. *I Am My Brother*. New York: Reynal & Co. Pp. 111–18.

PHELPS, GILBERT. *The Russian Novel in English Fiction*. London: Hutchinson & Co., 1956. Pp. 132–37, 191–92.

SEWARD, BARBARA. *The Symbolic Rose*. New York: Columbia University Press, 1960. Pp. 127–31.

SACKVILLE-WEST, V. *Encounter*, January, 1954.

———. "Virginia Woolf and Orlando," *Listener*, Jan. 27, 1955.

SIMON, IRENE. "Some Aspects of Virginia Woolf's Imagery," *English Studies* (Holland), Vol. XLI, No. 3 (June, 1960), pp. 180–96.

STEPHEN, ADRIAN. *The "Dreadnought" Hoax*. London: Hogarth Press, 1936.

Times Literary Supplement. "The Air of Bloomsbury," August 20, 1954. "The Perpetual Marriage," July 4, 1958. "Diversity and Depth," by Angus Wilson, Aug. 15, 1958.

TURNELL, MARTIN. *Modern Literature and Christian Faith*. London: Darton, Longman & Todd, 1961. Passages on D. H. Lawrence, E. M. Forster, and V. Woolf.

WOOLF, LEONARD. *Sowing: An Autobiography of the Years 1880 to 1904*. London: Hogarth Press, 1960.

Index

Brigid Broghy:

"V.W. brought to English prose an ear quite outstandingly defective, with the result that onomatopoeia cannot make good the imprecision of her images."

"V.W. was a clever and thoughtful literary person. Her sense of humour was genuine, though self-conscious: too much pondered, it comes out ponderous."

"V.W. may not deserve the compliment which the existence of Dr. Brewster's book implies, but neither does she deserve the insult of its execution."

"The only charming part of Dr. Brewster' book is on the jacket —— the photograph by Man Ray which, touched with surrealist insight, makes V.W. resemble a large, lost dragonfly."